Jeff Taylor

Recognized as an innovator and visionary in both the Internet and careers industries, Jeff Taylor has reinvented the way the world looks for employment. His "monster idea," conceived at the dawn of the World Wide Web, quickly became one of the first dot-com companies (454th on the Web) and has since grown into the world's leading online career site. Today, the Monster global network consists of local content and language sites in twenty-three countries and serves more than 50 million registered users, with over 20 million unique visitors monthly. Jeff is a frequent speaker at colleges and universities across the country, and at technology, advertising, and human capital conferences hosted by such noted organizations as Forrester Research, 21st Century Workforce Summit, The Partnership for Public Service, The Society for Human Resource Management (SHRM), Fast Company, and The Working Women Network. He serves on both the national and Massachusetts boards of directors of Junior Achievement and is also a board member of Boston's Wang Center for the Performing Arts. Jeff has an undergraduate degree from the University of Massachusetts at Amherst; holds a certificate from the Owner/President Management (OPM) Program, Executive Education, Harvard Business School; and has an Honorary Doctorate from Bentley College. In March 2000, Jeff reached yet another notable milestone: he became the Blimp Water-skiing World Champion.

Doug Hardy

A certified job and career transition coach, Doug Hardy was the editor-in-chief of Monster.com and is currently general manager of Monster Careers. Prior to joining Monster, Hardy directed book, magazine, and Web publishing businesses in New York and Boston.

Both Taylor and Hardy live near Boston.

monster®
Careers:

NETWORKING

Make the Connections That Make Your Career

BY JEFF TAYLOR,
FOUNDER OF monster®

WITH DOUG HARDY

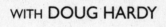

PENGUIN BOOKS

PENGUIN BOOKS

Published by the Penguin Group

Penguin Group (USA) Inc., 375 Hudson Street, New York, New York 10014, U.S.A.

Penguin Group (Canada), 90 Eglinton Avenue East, Suite 700, Toronto, Ontario, Canada M4P 2Y3 (a division of Pearson Penguin Canada Inc.)

Penguin Books Ltd, 80 Strand, London WC2R 0RL, England

Penguin Ireland, 25 St Stephen's Green, Dublin 2, Ireland (a division of Penguin Books Ltd)

Penguin Group (Australia), 250 Camberwell Road, Camberwell, Victoria 3124, Australia (a division of Pearson Australia Group Pty Ltd)

Penguin Books India Pvt Ltd, 11 Community Centre, Panchsheel Park, New Delhi–110 017, India

Penguin Group (NZ), cnr Airborne and Rosedale Roads, Albany, Auckland 1310, New Zealand (a division of Pearson New Zealand Ltd)

Penguin Books (South Africa) (Pty) Ltd, 24 Sturdee Avenue, Rosebank, Johannesburg 2196, South Africa

Penguin Books Ltd, Registered Offices:
80 Strand, London WC2R 0RL, England

First published in Penguin Books 2006

10   9   8   7   6   5   4   3   2   1

LIBRARY OF CONGRESS CATALOGING-IN-PUBLICATION DATA
Taylor, Jeff, 1960–
    Monster careers. Networking / by Jeff Taylor with Doug Hardy.
        p.   cm.
    ISBN 0-14-303601-7
    1. Business networks.   2. Interpersonal relations.   3. Social networks.
    4. Success in business.   5. Career development.   6. Job hunting.   I. Hardy, Doug.   II. Title.   III. Monster careers.

    HD69.S8T39   2006
    658'.044—dc22   2005049346

Printed in the United States of America
Set in Giovanni Book with Gill Sans
Designed by Heather Saunders

To Kay and Clark Taylor

ACKNOWLEDGMENTS

Many friends and colleagues contributed their time, expertise, and personal career network connections to this book. We'd particularly like to thank the following:

Dave Asprey	Peter Hutto
Wendy Babson	Ina Levin
Matt Bud	Carol McCarthy
Bob Burg	Ivan Misner
Jason Butler	Fred Nothnagel
Tom Cern	Cheri Paulson
Ian Christie	Susan RoAne
Lisa Cornay-Albright	John Rossheim
Johanna Cornwell	Caryn Saitz
Diane Darling	Patti Salvucci
Lisa Dennis	Michael Schutzler
Janice Dilworth	Peter Segal
Keith Ferrazzi	Robin Schwartz
Stephen Harper	Matthew Temple
Felix Heimberg	Peter Vogt
J. Scott Hoyland	

Once again, agent Peter Ginsberg acted as both expert advisor and trusted friend. Editors Brett Kelly (in her ever-increasing role) and Jane von Mehren never failed to make a book we thought was pretty good much better. And as ever, the employees, job seekers, and employer customers of Monster remain the network that counts.

CONTENTS

INTRODUCTION

You may think you're doing everything to find a job, but if you're reading this book, I'll assume it isn't going as well as you had hoped. You have sent out your resume, you're looking at job postings online, and you're asking everyone you know if they've heard of an open job position. But you still haven't landed. And you've heard that networking is the best way to find a job, but you don't know how to start.

I spend a lot of time talking to job seekers and employers, and I've discovered that, of all the tools available to land a great job, networking is probably the most misunderstood.

Some people hear "networking" and imagine themselves clutching a drink in a crowd, almost unable to breathe, searching for a friendly face among strangers. Others think they can go to a conference, grab three business cards, and land a job. Still others imagine that "networking" means passing a resume to a company president at a children's soccer game.

When those scenarios don't turn into a job, these people think, "Well, I gave it a try, but networking doesn't work for me."

The biggest myth of networking is the belief that extroverted, gregarious personality types are the only good networkers. But in fact, anyone can adapt networking to their individual style. I'll talk about four distinctive networking styles throughout the book.

In *Monster Careers* and its companion book, *Monster Careers: Interviewing*, I wrote that your most important career assets are your skills, experience, and personal culture. To those assets I'll add one more: your career network. In the new "free agent" world of work, your career advancement depends on your network. Your network will help you find a job *and* get that job done once you've landed it. To some extent, we're all products of our networks: Throughout our careers, we've met people who moved us along, either as connections to new jobs, as colleagues, or as friends. And the same has been true in our lives outside of work.

This book spells out a simple program to get your career network under way. It's focused on networking to locate a new job, and if you go on to weave networking activities into your daily life, you may never look for a job again. Instead, your network will bring jobs to your attention as part of your regular routine. You will hear about job opportunities, help others find work, and strengthen your ties to colleagues. Great networking never really ends.

Wherever you are in your career, you can build a web of relationships that will sustain you for the rest of your working life. Put the advice in this book into practice, and you will see yourself at the center of a bright and active career network. Good luck!

—JEFF TAYLOR

ABOUT THIS BOOK

L ike its predecessors *Monster Careers: How to Land the Job of Your Life* and *Monster Careers: Interviewing,* this book combines an A–Z description of specific job-hunting skills with written exercises, tips, and advice from masters of the game—in this case, the world's best networkers.

The written exercises are fundamental to building a career network. I've also created activities under the rubric "TRY THIS." These activities are meant to shake up your networking program from time to time; to help you dig deeper into your network, become more disciplined, or just make it fun. **Take the time to do these exercises and activities,** because reading about networking is not the same as doing it. The more you do, the easier it gets, and the more your career network seems to take on a life of its own.

Monster Careers: Networking also contains archetypes of four networking styles; they're explained briefly in chapter 1, they appear as characters in a narrative story line, and they're revisited at length in the Appendix. These archetypes illustrate the key differences in networking styles, but they are not to be confused with data-based "personality theory" in its various forms. They are meant to help you identify the strengths and shortcomings in your own style.

There's no limit to how far you can go with networking. The skills you learn in order to network effectively carry you beyond career, because networking is an open-ended life skill. The web of relationships you build when you're looking for a job will support you later as you do your job, and will inevitably become part of your social, community, and personal life.

Connecting

D oes the thought of using the connections you make in ordinary life to find a job make you nervous? Welcome to the majority. Even people who are convinced that networking *is* the thing to do (and 90 percent of job seekers say they intend to use networking) often don't know where to start. It's one of those skills that are just not taught in school. This is a shame, because career networking isn't magic—it can be learned like any skill.

You are about to develop a full set of habits and insights that will help you connect memorably. You'll learn to recognize and use the most fruitful connections (but not abuse them), and you'll create a personal network-management system to sustain momentum in your career.

This is strategic career work. Yes, networking will help you land your next job, but all accomplished networkers say the real power of connections is realized over years. Great networkers tell me that they are in the networking game for life, and it feeds their careers in unexpected ways time after time. Their networking constantly opens interesting new doors. For the best networkers, connecting becomes a way of life.

If you want to be an effective networker, you have to internalize the tips and techniques you'll learn here, and adapt them to your personal style. To help you do that, this book follows the stories of four fictional characters—Martin, Sarah, Luis, and Michelle—who represent four different styles of networking. I've named these four styles after four animals that typify them:

The Swan (Martin) is introverted and quiet, the kind of person whose natural inclination is to stay at home. Not a "natural networker," the Swan's ability to organize and focus on a step-by-step plan can make his networking very efficient. Swans would rather have one meaningful conversation than ten sessions of small talk.

The Butterfly networker (Sarah) meets new people all the time— the raw material for a great career network—but flits from one contact to another, rarely pausing to develop a deeper work relationship. Butterfly-style networkers have a great head start but need to learn about organization and follow-up.

The Dolphin (Luis) is my term for a networker who balances meeting new people and nurturing the relationships they already have. Their networking tends to be active and comfortable—so much so that networking sometimes appears to crowd out other activities!

The Lion (Michelle) focuses on forming just a few deep relationships. They may be introverted or they may have very intense work lives (time-pressed executives are often in this position). Lions can be very effective, but miss opportunities outside of their areas of focus.

These four archetypes appear in this book to show you that different people can approach networking in entirely different ways and be equally successful. As you read, ask yourself which style seems most natural to you (or possibly which blend of styles is most comfortable for you. Maybe you're a swan in big groups and a lion when you're meeting someone one-to-one). Look for the tips and techniques that play to your strengths. In addition to telling the stories of Martin, Sarah, Luis, and Michelle, I'll mention throughout the book how different networking styles might operate. After you've studied the complete networking plan, read the Appendix on page 153 called "Different Styles, Different Strengths." It presents more detailed descriptions of these networking styles, their advantages and pitfalls.

Sarah Needs a Network

Sarah set two cups of coffee on the kitchen table, and seated herself next to Michelle in the sunny breakfast nook. Michelle continued to study Sarah's resume.

"I'm doing everything," said Sarah. "I'm sending out resumes, calling headhunters, e-mailing job applications. But I never get an answer. Sometimes I think every resume I send gets the delete key."

"This resume looks great," said Michelle. "So why aren't you getting to the starting line?"

"That's just it. I don't know," said Sarah. "I have experience, I've had successes, and I even have references all set to tell employers how great I am. I know I can sell myself to an employer . . . but I never get face-to-face with anyone. I called the heads of HR at a couple of companies, and asked for a conversation, but their assistants all called back saying, 'just send us your resume.'" Sarah paused. "My problem is that I'm lousy at selling myself. That's why I thought you could give me some pointers."

"I train sales reps; I'm not a career counselor," said Michelle.

"I don't need counseling, Michelle," replied Sarah. "I know what I want to do, and thirty companies nearby must need my skills. I just have to get my foot in the door, that's all. My problem is that I don't know anyone."

"Wait a minute—you know all kinds of people," Michelle said. She continued, "Look how you behave at parties—Sarah, you can talk the knob off a door."

"That's just it," said Sarah. "I love to talk to people, I'm a total butterfly at a party, but when I ask for a job, I don't know what to say."

"How much networking have you done?"

"Not that, please. Everyone says I should try networking, but I hate the idea of cold calling strangers and asking for a job," Sarah said. She took the resume from Michelle. "Besides," she said, "I don't want to be pushy."

"So be the butterfly you are, and work out from there," said Michelle.

"What do you mean?"

"Butterflies typically know a lot of people, but not well enough. Do you have an address book?" asked Michelle. Sarah nodded. "Bring it here."

Sarah rummaged in her briefcase and produced a silver handheld PDA. "So far, it has eighty-five names, everyone from old employers to my mom." She sighed. "I thought I could make a network out of this, but I look at the list and think, 'I can't ask all these people for a job.'"

Michelle considered this. "Sarah, any good sales rep could see you have two problems. The first is your point of view. You see yourself standing alone and begging all these people for help. I see you at the center of an enormous web of relationships that you can use to benefit other people, and locate opportunities at the same time.

"The second problem," she continued, "is that you're confusing a list of names with a network. A list is dead. It has no energy, no connections, and no life. But if you pour energy into making that list more than just contacts, you'll be amazed at what happens." She tapped the PDA. "The more you put into these relationships, the faster you'll get a job." Michelle flipped open her cell phone. "In fact, there's someone I want you to meet, my business partner Luis."

Career Networking

A strong personal network will help you in any job search situation. If you're a new graduate and think you don't know anyone who can connect you to a job, you can still build a network. If you're changing careers, the people you know (even in your old profession) can get you into a new employer's office. If you've worked in the same job for twenty years, you're faced with a choice when the time comes to look: get help connecting with a new job, or go it alone.

A career network is nothing more or less than your unique collection of relationships. You already have the core of a career network— your relatives, friends, and professional acquaintances—that I call your *comfort network*. From that core, you can branch out and work to create a broad and vibrant web of relationships that will help you through many stages of your career.

If you are currently unemployed and have no career network, then you'll have to double down to create one as fast as possible. Unfortunately, the hardest time to build your network is when you really need it (it's like stringing up a safety net after you've fallen). However, if you're in this situation, the only thing to do is to get started today! The good news is that you have much more time than someone working full-time to start a lifelong career network—one that will find you a job this time, and the next, and the next.

If you are currently employed, you still need to get your network going. The time will come when you are out of work or considering a change. So, you need to network all the time; make it as much a part of your job as checking the e-mail.

The Advantages of Networking

Networking puts you ahead in the job search game in many ways:

Networking separates you from the pack. Let's say you're a college senior, and you go to the campus career center to begin a job search. The career center is loaded with good information but perhaps

150 other seniors with almost exactly the same experiences and skills are looking at the same opportunities. Instead of joining the crowd, you break out and contact the people you know, from family members to people in business your own research has discovered. It may take a little more work to get in front of people who can hire you, but often you're the one who gets to them first—or the only one who bothers to talk to them at all.

Networking works hand in hand with job applications. Your dream job is listed online. Fifty people write a cover letter that begins "Dear Sir or Madam. . . ." But if you've talked to someone in that company you can write: "Dear Mary, I saw this job on your company Web site and it reminded me of our conversation in your office last summer. . . ." Then Mary drops a note to the hiring manager saying, "Watch for this person's job application."

Networking catches you when you fall. A large, well-kept network is available to help you locate and land a new job if you are laid off or your employer disappears. If your network is active, you'll shorten your next job search by weeks—even months.

Networking uncovers hidden opportunity. Matt Bud, chairman of The Financial Executives Networking Group (FENG), points out that "when you're networking you're often not competing with anybody, because there was no job until you walked in the door for a conversation. Perhaps an employer has an opportunity he never recognized until you pointed it out. Perhaps there's a problem they haven't gotten around to solving—until you come along."

Networking opens up new possibilities. Talking to a wide range of people exposes you to a wide range of jobs. This is important if you're just starting out in your career. It's essential if you're considering a career change, because you will need to learn more about new job possibilities in a hurry, and you'll need to make connections outside your current circle.

Networking addresses the emotional side of hiring. Career center director Wendy Babson points out that "when it finally comes down to two equally skilled candidates, the employer hires the candidate who is a better fit with the company culture," she says. "If you've come to the interview through someone's referral, that person might say, 'You know, at the PTA, where I met him, he always volunteers for the hardest job, and he always comes through on a commitment.' This is really powerful information, and hard to find out about a candidate who comes in without a referral."

Networking makes you more valuable to the employer. Someone joins a new company, and eighteen months later they've brought in three top performers they know. None of them applied for a job—their relationship with the first person recommended them. What employer wouldn't want that?

According to outplacement executive Fred Nothnagel, the process of networking itself makes you more interesting to employers. "You talk with someone and learn something valuable; you go to the next person and you share what you found out; you learn more and soon you're taking the conversation to a higher level. They say, 'Here's a person who really knows his or her stuff. We've got to find a place for him before the competition does.'"

Relationships Matter More Than Ever

Relationships have always been central to work, whether for making decisions in the boardroom or getting a new customer into your shop. Master networker Keith Ferrazzi, author of *Never Eat Alone*, comments that "if you continue to manage relationships [they will] be available for you when you go back out into the job market three years from now. They'll make your next job hunt faster and easier."

In the past, a person stayed with one company or industry for their entire career. In the new world of work, everyone is a free agent. Corporate job security is over. Even if you stay with a single employer for a long time, you have to be prepared to switch jobs as business conditions change. A web of relationships, maintained throughout your career, goes with you when you leave.

In the past, the organization created your network. You were an IBM employee, living in a world of IBM relationships. Now, it's up to the individual to create the network. Long-term career relationships outside your current employer are part of your career survival kit: even if your address and job title shift every three years, your network of relationships can last a lifetime.

Outside of work, you're constantly involved in all sorts of social networks (more about these in chapters 3 and 6), and information passes freely among you and your acquaintances. There's a catch, though: Have you ever noticed that negative information, such as the fact that someone lost a job, seems to travel very fast, but good news, such as the fact that someone talented is suddenly available, travels more slowly? Maybe it's just the nature of gossip, but it's up to you to get your good news out there.

The Internet is also new in the grand scheme of things, and it has changed the speed at which we communicate and share information as well as how we think about our careers. Communication is the heart of the Internet. After ten years of intense development at a corporate level, Internet communication is beginning to bring its efficiencies and reach to the individual through e-mail, networking Web sites, personal Web sites and Web logs, wireless communications, and high-powered research.

Today, you can make contact with pretty much anyone else. Internet technologies help you find people with similar interests, identify common ground, connect, and follow up. You share the best of your work. You break down barriers of time, space, and status.

A Web of Relationships

Just contacting someone, however, isn't enough to get a job. You can connect with anyone, but you don't have time to develop a relationship with everyone. The most critical factor in career networking is not making contacts but creating and nurturing a high-quality **web of relationships.** You need to be remembered by people who can either hire you, or introduce you to someone who can hire you. As Patti Salvucci of the networking organization Business Network International (BNI) puts it, "It's not who you know but *who you meet through who you know.*" People don't make introductions for a complete stranger.

When you're building career-networking relationships, you want people to have a positive point of view about you:

- Are you who you say you are?
- Do they know your skills, strengths, and weaknesses?
- Can they describe you clearly and briefly to another person?
- Are you helpful to them?
- Do you follow through on your commitments?
- Are you accountable for your mistakes?
- Are you someone they feel comfortable with?

When you have a relationship with someone who answers each of these questions with a yes, you can have a good career-networking relationship.

How many of these relationships will you need to get a job? There's no way to put a number on that, because while career networking is—point blank—one of the best ways to get a job, it is more a set of lifelong habits than a onetime project.

Your web of relationships practically defines your career progress, says master networker Keith Ferrazzi: "A career can be viewed as a series of people that have made you successful. The raise that you want—somebody has to say you're worth more money. The promotion you earned—some person has to decide you should be promoted. That next job—there is a man or a woman out there who will make the decision whether you're hired or not."

You might have to put a good deal of time and energy into it, but even if you could meet just one new person every week you'd add fifty people into your network every year. And that web of relationships, if carefully maintained, will be there for you when you need it.

You Know More People Than You Think

If you're one of those folks who thinks they don't know anybody, it's time to change your point of view about the networking numbers game. The truth is you've probably had forty opportunities in the past forty days to connect with people you don't know, and if you're like most of us, you let thirty-nine of them walk right on by.

A typical person actually knows at least a hundred people well enough to talk on a first-name basis. Each of those people knows 100 additional people. In a strictly academic sense, you're one referral away from 10,000 people! Not every one will have a job connection for you, of course, and you don't have time to meet 10,000 people before you land a job, but I want to make the point that your actual universe of potential job contacts is larger than you might realize. A good networking program helps you continuously identify those individuals who can connect you to a job. (Incidentally, if you think you don't know 100 people, I'll prove it to you in chapter 3!)

This is the second phase of the numbers game. Networking builds high-quality connections all along the way to your next job. Scattering resumes here and there doesn't. That's why, even though it takes more time than other techniques, networking is actually an efficient activity in a job search.

Let's look at networking math on an achievable scale: Over the course of five weeks you contact 100 people—4 a day. If each of them has just 2 potential contacts for you—you'll have 200 new job connections in addition to your first 100. Total: 300.

And what if each of those 200 new contacts could introduce you to just 1 new person? Now 500 people know you're looking for a job . . . and they learned it from a trusted friend or colleague.

Does this sound like a lot of work? It is, at first. Like most good work, it takes a while to build momentum, but this is how it gets done.

Two Critical Qualities

Think about the times you watched a movie or bought a product because a friend recommended it. You trusted your friend's recommendation and you followed through on it.

That first quality, **trust,** is one foundation of effective networking. Trust is fragile and irreplaceable. When you ask someone to refer you for a job, you're asking them to put their reputation on the line. They won't do that if they doubt you.

In a networking relationship, *sincerity* and *reliability* create trust. I'll remind you of this throughout the book because it bears repeating many times: Career networks fall apart because people violate someone's trust, through either insincerity or lack of follow-up. Don't fall into these network-killing traps! Demonstrate sincerity and reliability without fail.

The second must-have quality of your networking program is **commitment.** You have to be in it for the long haul. If you are committed to building a career network, you'll weave it into your daily life. When you tell someone you'll call next week—call next week. When you promise to refer someone to a new contact, make that referral within twenty-four hours.

Career networking is like maintaining your health—it works better if you do it a little bit every day. People who start networking every time they switch jobs but don't stick to it in the interim are like the folks who exercise and diet for two weeks because the doctor ordered them to lose weight, but then drop the healthy lifestyle until the next crisis.

Commitment means you'll make a habit of pouring your energy into that web of relationships. It means you will do what it takes to overcome shyness, fear, or procrastination. You don't have to change your personality to make a commitment. Commitment isn't the ability to do everything perfectly—it's the willingness to keep doing things until you get better at them.

You Don't Have to Be a Natural

Very few people are instantly good at this work, but you don't have to be a natural salesman, a professional actor, or a trial lawyer to network well. As long as you are trustworthy and committed, you'll get results. And you will get better at it quickly. As you form professional relationships, you'll very soon see the strengths of the self-description I call your "personal brand," your conversational style, and your follow-up.

You might have to push yourself out of your comfort zone a little just to follow the early steps. Keep the reward in mind: more business relationships, more opportunity, a shorter job search, and a better job!

For those of you who say that you just can't stand networking: I suspect that behind this feeling are some excuses or false beliefs that need to be challenged. Let's talk back to those objections:

"I don't have time to network." If you're in a job search, you don't have time **not** to network. Sending your resume out, researching companies, applying online for jobs . . . each of these requires information and connections, and networking provides both. If you are working now, you'll have to make it part of your daily or weekly routine and you have the luxury of a long lead time so that, when the inevitable next job search comes, you'll have a vibrant network ready to find you a job.

"I don't know anybody." Not anybody? A sibling, a parent, a neighbor, a librarian, a schoolmate, a former colleague, a former boss, a teacher? You probably mean you don't know anybody who has a job opening waiting for you. Nobody does when they start networking. A career network is a net that catches opportunities when they appear.

"I don't know how to start." You'll find many ways to connect with people throughout this book. The Internet has made this work much easier than it used to be. Remember—it's not just contact, it's the relationship that makes the difference. In chapters 3 and 4, I'll show you a "low-impact" way to start.

"Nobody wants to talk to me." If you mean, "Nobody wants me to bug them for a job," you're right. However, people will want to talk to you about prospects if you give them good reason to. In addition, people like to be heard, and good networking makes you an incredible listener.

"I have nothing of value to offer." Diane Darling, CEO of Effective Networking, contradicts this common assumption of first-time networkers by pointing out you have your network to offer. "Your contacts might want a vacation suggestion—and your aunt is a travel agent. They might need to find an immigration attorney,

and your tennis partner knows one. They might want to hear the inside story about the private school your college roommate attended. Making these connections for people is what I call third-party networking. Other people may have the answer to their problem, but you make the connection, and *you* get the visibility."

"I have no power." Real power is the ability to make things happen. Put your energy into your career network and I guarantee you, things will happen. Don't worry about not having pull or influence today; if you have something of value to offer, and the drive to get things in motion, that's power enough for now.

"I'm too shy; I can't talk to people." Shyness can be a huge stumbling block for many. There's no avoiding the fact that you have to communicate with people. And if one-on-one phone and face time is a major difficulty for you, Internet technologies (see chapter 7) can make networking less painful. Sometimes you still have to get face-to-face with people, but even if you're the most solitary introvert on Earth you can learn to reach out.

"I just need a job, not a new set of chores to do." It takes hard work to land a new job or make progress in your career. The beauty of career networking is that after you get a job, you can adapt the skills you've learned to help you do the job better, and to advance your nonwork life. None of your effort is wasted.

There will always be an excuse handy for why you don't network, but at the end of the day you have to find the self-motivation to do it. If you just wait for something to happen, nothing will happen. You can read this book, but if it doesn't result in you reaching out to other people, you won't see results. If you take one of the practical, how-to tips of this book—even just one —and get into motion you'll make things happen.

EXERCISE 1

Your Web of Relationships

You already sit at the center of a web of relationships, which you'll actively expand as you network toward a job. To get an idea of how this works, draw the following example.

Write your name in the center of a piece of paper, then write the names of three or four people you know—friends, schoolmates, coworkers, and the like. Connect your name with each person, and note the nature of the relationship. Your drawing might look like this:

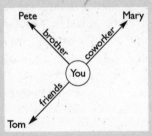

Now expand the connections by naming a friend, relative, or coworker of each friend you listed, like this:

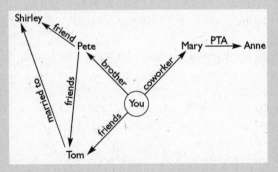

There's already some overlap here—your brother Pete is friends with Tom and his wife, Shirley. Thus you connect to Shirley through two people.

Now if you really want to see how the web works, add a friend, relative, or coworker to each of the new names, and fill in every relationship you know, like this:

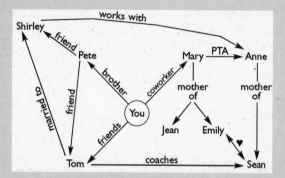

In this example, Anne works at an employer who might hire you. You connect with her through Tom, Shirley, or Mary.

Draw this web a few times with different names, and you'll see that you are completely surrounded by connections to potential employers. The first set of people will lead you to the second, and they'll lead you to another set, and so on. **Any of them might connect you to a job or another person who is hiring.**

This web will soon expand beyond your ability to draw it (unless you use a 10-foot whiteboard!). You can make dozens of connections like these from your existing relationships, using the plan described in chapters 3 and 4.

Keep this image in mind, and look for these connections as you build your career network. It's not just a list of contacts—it's a **web of relationships.**

Someone has to put you in contact with your next employer. You can do a lot on your own with resumes and job applications, but even then, there's plenty of competition before the final candidates are selected for a job interview. Networking puts the power of human relationships on your side.

Luis Asks Three Questions

"Sarah, meet Luis," said Michelle.

Luis shook Sarah's hand and said, "It's good to meet you, Sarah. I'm looking forward to helping you, if I can." They walked into the office that Michelle shared with Luis.

Sarah was surprised at Luis's appearance. Michelle had described him as a master networker, someone who had hundreds of well-kept connections, and Sarah had an image in her mind of a polished executive. Luis looked more like a private-school English teacher, with his blazer, striped tie, and nylon briefcase. His thick glasses made Luis's eyes overlarge in his face.

"Let's walk through your job search so far," said Luis, offering a chair.

For ten minutes, Sarah reviewed the steps she'd taken—polishing a resume, researching the local job market, applying for jobs. She described her early networking attempts, which had failed to turn up any job leads.

When she was finished, Luis said, "I understand your frustration, Sarah. You definitely need a structured plan to move networking into your job search."

Sarah nodded. "Okay, but Michelle said networking's not the same as asking for a job. I can talk to all the people I want, but unless I ask for a job, how can I find where the jobs are?"

"Good question," said Luis. "Let's talk about how connections get made. I'm going to ask you three questions. First, can you think of a time you wanted two people to meet—a time when you just knew they'd have a lot to talk about?"

"I can think of a dozen," said Sarah. "Half the fun of going to a party is pulling one person over to another and saying, 'You two have just *got* to meet.'"

"Good. Michelle said you were like that. Next question: How did you know they'd have a lot to talk about?"

"It's just my instinct, I guess . . ." Sarah started, and then she paused. "Wait. It's not as simple as that." Luis peered over his glasses, smiling, and Sarah continued. "I knew a lot about each person. I could list five things they had in common."

Luis said, "Right—you knew a lot about each person." He leaned forward and asked in a conspiratorial whisper, "Third question—what did *you* get out of putting them together?"

"It was fun! I feel special when people hit it off," said Sarah.

"Right, Sarah. You brought people together, and you felt good. Maybe they'd get along. Maybe they'd become friends . . . or more, perhaps?" Luis said with mock seriousness. Sarah grinned back, and Luis continued, "In the job-hunting business, that's called a referral: one person is the employer and the other is the candidate, but in the way it works, it's really no different from introducing two people at a party."

Michelle said, "The good news is, more jobs are filled by referrals than any other single source. Your goal when you're networking is to give—and get—referrals."

"How will I do that?" asked Sarah.

Luis answered, "By systematically reaching out, having conversations, and being helpful. That's how Michelle and I have found our best clients, and that's how you'll find an employer. Or rather, how they'll find you."

Rules for Referrals

Picture this: A manager has received six similar resumes for an open job position. One comes with a note from a colleague, which says "I know this person and I think you should know them, too!"

If you think that resume gets the most consideration, you're right. The others may have potential, but nothing more. An existing relationship puts that candidate ahead in the competition for the job.

Career networking seeks to generate *referrals* like this. A referral happens when someone recommends you to someone else. There are three principles that encourage referrals.

Principle #1: If you are clear about who you are and what value you bring to an employer, people can pass that along. Here are two examples of the referrals you want to generate (a person you know is talking to an employer):

"Oh, if you're having trouble with your warehouse operation, you have to talk to this guy I know named Bob Thomas. He's fixed that problem before."

"Tom, you told me last week you're expanding your athletics program. You ought to talk to Mary Green at the Walt Whitman School over in Knoxville, because she led their athletics expansion two years ago. She'll be able to tell you how she did it."

Principle #2: People refer people they know, like, and trust. This is unscientific, subjective, and maybe even unfair, but it's also true. The most sincere referrals have a positive emotional foundation.

The opposite is also true: people who dislike, disrespect, or don't trust you aren't going to help. Now, what people think about you is not entirely within your control. Maybe they don't like short people, or people who went to your college, or people with your accent. If you discover this about someone in your network, move on.

Principle #3: A key way to generate referrals is to give them. Dr. Ivan Misner, CEO of Business Network International, describes top networkers as "connectors—people in the community who everyone goes to for information or connections with other people. The way to become a connector is to help people solve their problems, and sometimes that's just a matter of bringing together a person with a need or problem with a person who can solve that problem."

Companies Love Referrals

Today, leading corporations try to get as much as 30 percent of their workforce from referrals. Companies love to find a new employee through an existing employee's referral because it's such an effective screen. The current employee already knows a lot about you, and a lot about the company's culture, values, and job requirements, which helps to ensure a good fit.

When I meet an interesting person, I don't always have an open job in mind, but I ask myself if they might be good in my company because I recognize an intellectual or cultural fit. Some top-performing employees are discovered in casual conversations.

Employers large and small are now actually training recruitment and HR staff to network, and also are offering rewards to their employees for referrals: "Refer someone, and if they get hired, we'll pay you a $1,000 bonus." Early studies show that employees who arrive by referral are more likely to remain and succeed.

The direct connection results in better hires. And referrals are cheap, even when an employer pays for them. A thousand-dollar bounty on a good candidate is a bargain compared to traditional methods of finding candidates such as newspaper advertising.

Why don't employers use referrals for *all* their hiring? It would be nice, but a variety of pressures make this impossible. Effective referrals require judgment on the part of the employee. Employees may not know anyone with the right set of skills for a particular job. There's also time pressure—if you are an HR director with the task of hiring twenty-five new sales representatives in three months, you cannot rely solely on a referral program; you need to hire fast, and you will use all available methods, but those in the referral pool will undoubtedly have an advantage.

Recruiters Love Referrals, Too

Maybe you'll find a job through a professional recruiter or executive "headhunter." How do you think you'll connect with them? By sending a resume blindly in the mail? A good recruiter gets 200 resumes a day.

Instead, what if one of that recruiter's successful candidates referred you to them? When I owned a recruiting company, I interviewed candidates every day. If a candidate impressed me, I would always ask, "Who else is as skilled as you?" When I placed someone in a job, I'd say, "If someone really terrific confides in you that they're looking for work, send them my way and I might be able to help."

For a recruiter, successful candidates act as filters. They relieved me of endless hours of reading inappropriate, blind resumes. They recommended colleagues based on qualities that are very hard to judge in a resume, like trustworthiness, a good work ethic, or coolness under stress.

A few sharp candidates—real networkers—understood that sending an occasional referral to me was also a good way to remind me of them as well. If candidate A referred candidate B to me, I not only paid close attention to B but remembered A's favor. Two or three years later, when candidate A decided it might be time to move into a new job, did I take their call? You bet I did.

In this positive atmosphere, I'd also ask candidates to recommend me to their friends. Some of them brought me my best candidates— people who were already happily employed and weren't sending their resumes out, but were open to new opportunities and highly experienced and desirable to employers. I realized that a relationship with a first-rate candidate could result in many placements with his or her friends over the years. That's another reason why recruiters love referrals.

So, for a recruiter, hiring manager, or Human Resources professional, networking saves time, builds new business, and burnishes a reputation.

Going Around, Coming Around

In *Monster Careers*, I said there's a karmic payback in offering your help to others. I also said that your attitude is hugely important in a job search.

Discard the idea that, because your goal is to get a job, there's something strictly self-serving about this. It's fine to expect a payoff for your career networking—a job, a new client, a new opportunity—but it's not always possible to know what that payoff will be. The highest form of career networking is engagement in the lives of the people in front of you—really listening, really coming to the conversation with good intentions and interest, compassion, and empathy, and really using your creativity and resources to help. Your reputation as a helpful person will always generate new contacts, and networking will organically become part of your life's work. If you are connecting people effectively, you will inevitably be connected to opportunity by them.

There may be no way to study this scientifically, but everyone who has worked a serious networking program, from the first-time job seeker to the real estate agent who works as a community volunteer, agrees that the people who offer service to others without directly seeking reward always find their kindness returned many times over. If you listen to people, and find out about their work, you can help them, with no immediate reward but inner satisfaction. (Actually, that's not a bad payoff.) They will remember you as helpful, trustworthy, and committed—and when the time comes, they will refer you to the right person.

You also have to rid yourself of the feeling that your networking is asking for charity, says Matt Bud, chairman of The Financial Executives Networking Group (FENG). "Men, especially, are reluctant to ask for a favor. Think of the last time you were able to help someone else. I bet it felt pretty good, right? Giving someone else a chance to help you is really doing them a favor, and that's the ultimate truth about networking."

Try This

When offering help, it's best to offer something you do well. So pretend someone's asking you for help, and list the kind of help that plays to your networking style's strengths. For example:

Swan: "I'll e-mail you a link to a helpful Internet site I discovered as part of my networking research." *(The swan is more comfortable with e-mail, and can be very thorough in his or her research.)*

Butterfly: "I know at least five people who have kids in that sport. Would you like to talk to one of them?" *(The butterfly can capitalize on a broad number of acquaintances.)*

Dolphin: "I might know someone who can help you. Tell me more while I look through my contact list." *(The dolphin makes connections readily, and has a broad number of contacts.)*

> **Lion:** "I have faced that business challenge, too. Let's have lunch and see if we can come up with some possible solutions." *(The lion digs deep into a problem and is very strong one-on-one.)*

Getting Under Way

In *The Psychology of Sales Call Reluctance*, George W. Dudley and Shannon L. Goodson note that the single behavior that distinguishes sales management superstars is not charm, persuasive power, or extroversion but a continuous investment in growth—growth in their tools, their teams, and themselves. It's the same for networking: the key to success is continuous investment in the tools and behaviors that foster growth of your network and your skills in managing it.

Now I'm going to ask you to begin that continuous investment. Go through the exercise below, and when you're done, get on with the Monster Careers networking plan. It begins in the next chapter.

EXERCISE 2

List Your Assets

You are starting out with more assets than you may realize. Before you begin the step-by-step networking plan in chapter 3, take a few minutes to complete this simple exercise as a warm-up for the work to come.

1. **Describe who you are and what you want.** This is a little preview of the "personal brand statement" in chapter 3. Write a paragraph describing your professional assets—your skills, experience, and personal traits that make you good at your work. Ask a trusted friend to read it and comment. Have you missed anything important?

2. Name five people you know, like, and trust. Beside each name, list answers to the following:
- How did you meet?
- Why do you trust them?
- What do you do to maintain these relationships?

3. Make a referral list. Be prepared to describe the skills, experience, or personal traits that help you enthusiastically connect them to other people:
- List three people you could recommend for a job (even if they're currently happily employed), and describe why you'd recommend them.
- List three additional people you could recommend to provide a service (lawyer, plumber, personal organizer, dentist, et al.). Describe why you chose them.
- List three people you know who have the ability to hire someone, or who work for prominent employers in your area.

Networking ca. 1921

Late in 1921, a man named Jim Pendergast brought his uncle Mike to a small, failing men's clothing store on 12th Street in Kansas City. Mike ran a sophisticated political organization, and Jim thought one of the store's owners might be a good candidate for county judge. Jim had seen the character of the man in combat in World War I. He had reason to remember the man: years earlier, the man had helped exonerate Lieutenant Pendergast in an Army inquiry about an accident that had killed three soldiers. Jim Pendergast knew that the man's store was failing, and he would be looking for another job.

When the two men offered their endorsement for the failing businessman to run for county judge, Harry Truman immediately accepted.

Incidentally, it was not just a lucky break that Truman knew Pendergast. According to David McCullough in his superb biography *Truman,* Lieutenant Truman "had been assigned to run the regimental canteen—a dispensary for candy, sodas, cigarettes, tobacco, shoelaces, writing paper—and it was this that soon made him known to nearly everyone in camp."

At the moment when Truman faced the worst prospects of his life—broke, middle-aged, frustrated, and failing—his personal qualities, reputation, and large web of relationships set him on a new path not only to success, but into history.

3 Start Close to Home

Good career networking is more like farming than hunting. Instead of hoping to hunt down that elusive open job requisition, you plant the seeds of awareness in many people's minds, and nurture them carefully. When a ripe opportunity appears (often before the job is advertised) your network drops it in your lap.

The steps in this chapter will show you how to begin a networking program, starting with the relationships you already have. These are your foundation, and they make the difference between success and failure over the long term.

First, you'll have to get organized. This is important because good networking requires that you know a lot of information about a lot of people, and an organized networking program makes that possible.

Then, you'll create a personal brand statement. This is a critical component, neglected by too many networkers. A personal brand statement makes it easy for other people to know who you are, what you offer employers, and how they can help you.

Finally in this chapter, you will map out your first conversations with your comfort network—the people you already know, but may not recognize as part of a career-networking program.

Along the way, you'll create a few tools that help make networking less strenuous, such as a contact management system and a networking kit of items to take along to meetings.

The Lion Stalks Her Prey

After five years in business, Michelle and Luis had established routines for locating new customers that played to each other's styles. It was 8 A.M., and as usual, Michelle was at her desk booting up her contact list. Also as usual, Luis the dolphin was off having breakfast with a customer, or a former customer, or someone who might lead him to a customer. Michelle was always impressed at his appetite for new acquaintances. His type had that in common with Sarah's butterfly style.

Michelle was also impressed—and sometimes appalled—at Luis's lack of visible organization. His desk was a shambles, with business cards stacked in piles and dozens of notes stuffed into folders. Yet somehow he managed to keep it all straight. He talked to everybody; he trusted his luck. Not her style.

Michelle believed that in networking, luck was something you planned, and this morning she was planning to be lucky. A friend had told her that the tech company named Chestnut Systems was about to expand its sales force, and that would be a great opportunity for new business. She studied her contact records for a connection to Chestnut. Finding none, she quickly wrote up an e-mail asking if anyone knew an employee there, and sent the e-mail to twenty people on her "A" list. Then, she turned to the event calendars of local organizations. Reading through the calendars, she saw that Chestnut

Systems was a corporate sponsor of the Beltway Networkers meeting the following week. Bingo.

Michelle went online to the Beltway Networkers' site, registered Luis and herself for the event, and then looked up Chestnut Systems' Web site. Cruising to the "About us" section, she studied the executive staff at Chestnut.

Sean Jordan, Senior Vice President of Sales. She had her target.

Make Networking a Daily Routine

Career networking is time-consuming, and it's hard to fit new projects into a busy life. It's important to ask yourself realistically: How much time can you dedicate to this in a week? If you're unemployed and working forty hours a week in a job search, at least a third of your time, or thirteen hours a week, should center on networking tasks. You can get a lot done in thirteen hours and still have plenty of time for other job search activities, like writing a resume or preparing for an interview. You can probably scratch three to six people off your list every day in the early weeks of a networking effort.

If you are currently employed, you should carve out enough time in a week to expand your network by two or three individuals—one call, e-mail, or letter a day, and one face-to-face conversation a week is probably ambitious enough. Your challenge is to weave networking into your weekly routine. This is the point at which a lot of good intentions fail in the face of a fifty-hour workweek, but there is no better time to build a career network than when you have a job. Make a simple commitment to devote one hour a day to your network— whether it's placing calls and catching up with e-mails, updating your contact info, making a drinks date with a friend from school, or having lunch with an old colleague. You'll gain momentum that will pay off the next time you switch jobs. (The best networkers make time for it every day, period.)

The next challenge is staying organized. In the first days and weeks of career networking, it's easy to remember who you spoke to, what

EXERCISE 3

Contact File
_____

Name: _____

Priority: ☐

Company/Organization: _____

Position: _____

Address: _____

_____

Phone: _____

E-mail: _____

Referred by/Found by: _____

Relationship: _____

What I can do for them: _____

Date met: _____

Meeting notes: _____

Follow-up: _____

Referred me to: _____

_____

I referred them to: _____

You can download this form at monstercareers.com

they said, what you promised you'd do, who they referred you to, etc. You could write it all on a scrap of paper. But as your network grows those scraps of paper add up—and pretty soon you're buried in scraps of paper.

The simplest and least expensive system is to make a record of each networking conversation. You can use the networking contact file below as a template. Simply copy the form (or download it to your computer at **monstercareers.com**) and fill out one after any networking conversation. Keep sheets organized in a file folder or three-ring notebook; you'll refer back to them often and they should be at your fingertips when, for example, you're trying to remember a connection your friend made for you two months ago.

The contact record contains essential contact information, a priority level for the contact, notes about the meeting, and reminders of commitments made. (All these items are covered in detail in the next chapters, so refer back to this sample for help in filling out your own contact records.)

Here's what a typical record will look like after a networking meeting.

Contact File

Name: Sam Jaworski
Priority: [A]
Company/Organization: Middletown Health Centers, Inc.
Position: Director of Information Systems
Address: 1212 Springfield Highway, Omaha NB 68127
Phone: 123-456-7890
E-mail: **sam@mhcinc.org**
Referred by/Found by: Mel Merritt
Relationship: Mel and Sam worked together at Memorial Hospital
What I can do for them: Share my network; discuss IT trends; refer others
Date met: January 16, 2006

Meeting Notes: No current positions open, but receptive. Liked my stories. MHC buying long-term care facilities and system integration is his big challenge. Told me to think about BPX certification.

Follow-up: 1/17/06 call Terry and Supriya (see below). 2/15/06 follow-up call.

Referred me to: At MHC: Ken Alderson (Tech Support) and Sally Campbell (HR). George Garibaldi at Bright Systems. Nan Johnson at Solvent.

I referred them to: Terry Walker (re: his experience with the people who are pitching Sam on a payroll-tracking package) and Supriya Shah (personal—Sam needs new vet for his three dogs!)

The next step up from do-it-yourself contact records is a notebook-type personal organizer. Many come with contact pages that can be used to keep track of your networking.

Moving up in sophistication (and expense), the popular handheld computers (PDAs) have address book applications to manage contacts. Use the "notes" areas in each contact file to save the information like that on the paper contact file.

At the top of the scale are contact management software programs (like ACT® or Goldmine®), which are designed for long-term business relationship management in jobs such as sales. They can be overwhelming for beginners, but they also can increase your productivity. If you like working with sophisticated software, and you're determined to keep your career network going beyond the goal of finding your next job, you might look into them.

However you choose to organize and store your information, early in your network building make a habit of recording who you talk to, their relationship to you, the referrals they give you, and any commitments you make to follow up with them. Do this even with very familiar people. Choose a method, device, or software you can use daily—your choice of tool is not as important as the habit of capturing the information. This is an important habit; it's the key to good follow-up, which in turn is the key to effective long-term networking. Whether you like to keep paper records or files, or prefer the latest contact management program or gadget, the key is to set up a system and use it, so make sure you're comfortable with whatever method you choose.

Get Your Story Together

You want every contact in your career network to have a clear idea of who you are, what you offer, and what you are looking for. I call this your "personal brand statement," and it's critical to getting effective referrals. Your contacts have to know this information in order to make the connections that lead you to a job.

How do you help people pass along this message? What do you say when a networking contact asks, "So tell me about yourself" or "I'd be happy to introduce you to my boss. What should I tell her about you?"

The answer is: Give them something simple! Prepare a fifteen-second personal brand statement with the key points you want your contacts to repeat:

1. Start with a single sentence describing what you do (or want to do) for a living.
2. Add your best "selling point" as an employee—your best talents, work skills, or outstanding work achievements.
3. Explain why you want to connect with other people.
4. Ask for referrals to anyone who may be connected to the work you seek.

For example, the personal brand statement for an advertising copywriter who is looking for a new job in direct marketing might contain the following: *(a) I'm a copywriter and I work at ABC ad agency; (b) I have written outstanding copy for successful broadcast and print campaigns; (c) I've decided to learn more about the direct-marketing business; (d) I want to talk to people who are involved in direct marketing.*

Notice the statement doesn't say: "I'm looking for a job." Instead, it focuses on something the next contact can deliver, and that is a referral. It's an invitation to talk about their work, their organization, their industry, and their contacts—and that information will lead you step-by-step toward job opportunities when they do open.

(Incidentally, when network contacts ask if you're looking for a job, you can say yes, in the long run—but you are not going to ask them for a job. You are going to ask them about their work, their knowledge, and their contacts. You are looking for connections to people who might know people who are hiring. This statement makes people more relaxed about helping you.)

Here are three more examples:

1. Mara: *(a) I'm an attorney who's experienced in litigation; (b) I've worked for a big downtown firm for five years, and have examples of my success; (c) I would like to change from litigation to family practice; (d) I want to meet partners in local law firms who do family practice.*

2. Kim: *(a) I was a marketing professional for three years in a midsize finance company in Toronto; (b) My marketing programs doubled our market share of the mortgage business; (c) I've moved to Chicago recently for personal reasons; (d) I'm looking for people connected to marketing in finance, banking, lending, and related firms.*

3. Morris: *(a) I'm a senior customer service manager; (b) I've run large customer service groups and twice organized new ones from the ground up; (c) I am looking for a new position in customer service management; (d) I want to talk to anyone connected to customer service at a senior level, in a company where service is genuinely important to the business.*

Draft a personal brand statement here—and then read it aloud. Does it sound like you? Is it memorable? As your networking grows, return to this statement from time to time. Is it still accurate and memorable? Your personal brand statement can change as your career network gives you new information and insights to the job possibilities in your area.[1]

---

[1] There's much more about building a personal brand statement in *Monster Careers: How to Land the Job of Your Life.*

Personal Brand Statement

What I do:

My best selling point(s):

Why I want to connect with others:

I want to talk to the following people:

People won't repeat your personal brand statement mechanically. They'll add their opinion and the reason they're passing you along to the next person. Show enthusiasm. If you don't believe in your value (expressed in your personal brand), how can you expect others to believe it? This is also why you need to back up your personal brand statement with the right attitude. People in your career network will form their own opinions of you based on your behavior. You can say you're reliable, but if you promise to call them Monday and then don't call until Friday, they'll doubt it. You can say you're a great salesman, but be prepared to back up your claim with stories of your best sales. Your behavior when networking will enhance that all-important personal brand.

Here's how the personal brand statement examples above get passed along the networking grapevine:

"Scott Johnson, a college friend of my son, is a copywriter who works at ABC ad agency. He has written outstanding copy for successful radio and print campaigns, and now he's decided to learn more about the direct-marketing business. He's looking to talk to people involved with that. **He's smart, trustworthy, and has a lot to offer any advertising agency—as a copywriter. I think you should talk to him.**"

"My friend Mara has been working in litigation at a downtown firm for five years, and now she is considering a change—moving into family practice. She's not going to pressure anyone for a job, but she does want to talk to trusted family practice lawyers and find out more about what it's like working at one of those firms. **She seems very solid to me. I don't know if you're hiring, but because your firm has been so great handling my dad's estate, I thought I'd refer her to you first."**

"Kim worked on marketing campaigns for financial products, mostly mortgages, at my last employer in Toronto. Now that she's moved to the area, she's talking to anyone who's connected with lenders in the area—banks, mortgage brokers, and the like. **Kim told me stories about how several times she marketed products like yours . . . didn't you say you would be beefing up your marketing staff in the next couple of months?"**

"Morris was a customer service manager for twenty years, and he's organized new customer service teams twice. He tells me he'd like to meet any person you know who appreciates customer service, and who may know someone at a business where that's a priority. **You have to talk to this guy. He's the most organized manager I've ever met . . . and between us, I think your customer service department could use that."**

Each one of these statements was passed along to a potential employer because the person speaking had a clear idea of someone's personal brand *and* a relationship with the next person.

List Your Comfort Network

You understand how real career networking leads to jobs. You've made a commitment to doing the work it takes to build a growing, vital web of relationships.

Now that you have something to say, it's time to figure out whom you'll say it to. The easiest place to recognize and hone good networking habits is the hidden social network you already possess— the familiar group of friends, family, and acquaintances I call your "comfort network." These are the people who will be most willing to help because you already have a relationship. For example, you probably have a network of required services in your life: a plumber, an electrician, a doctor, a dentist, a veterinarian, a painter. Similar groups revolve around your home, school, community, etc. These are all networks that you've helped to create and maintain already; you just may not have seen them as "networks" until now.

This is one of those initial decision points that gets networking off to the right start. If you haven't done much networking before, just making a list of your comfort network—remember, these are existing relationships—can show you how great the possibilities are.

You can begin just by writing the names of everyone you know. Don't stop until you have 100–200 names on the list. Use a computer, notebook, or whatever feels most comfortable to make this initial list—just keep writing.

Can't come up with 100 names? Here are three methods for creating that first list.

EXERCISE 5
Your Comfort Network—by Relationship

Try listing two or three people in each of the following categories:

   1. Family

   2. Friends

   3. Neighbors

   4. Your friends' parents

   5. Your parents' friends

   6. Your parents' colleagues

   7. Your children's friends' parents

   8. Classmates

   9. Alumni(ae) of any school you attended, including high school

   10. Members of the local chamber of commerce

11. Members of your church, temple, or other faith-based groups

12. Professors

13. Teachers

14. Mentors

15. Former bosses

16. Former or current colleagues

17. Former or current customers

18. Former employees who you managed

19. Members of the YMCA, YWCA, or other clubs

20. Members of professional groups to which you belong

21. Members of a service organization (e.g., the Rotary)

22. School committee members

23. Counselors

24. Friends from military service

25. Coaches (in sports, arts, hobbies, etc.)

26. Your doctor

27. Your lawyer

28. Your insurance agent

29. Your accountant or tax preparer

30. Your auto mechanic

31. The manager of your favorite coffee shop

32. The bartender at your favorite watering hole

33. The owner or maitre d' of your favorite restaurant

34. Your barber/hairstylist

35. Your mortgage broker

36. Your real estate broker

37. Your veterinarian

38. Your dry cleaner

39. Any shop or business owners who know you by name (especially in "high touch" businesses like art dealers, florists, dress shop managers, wedding planners, wine dealers—people who have long conversations with others)

40. Any acquaintance who owes you a favor

Right away, you may be inclined to leave some of the closest people in your life off the list, either because you think you know all the same people or because you're afraid you will somehow abuse the relationship. Felix Heimberg, a recruiting and staffing manager at HiLine Inc., says that's a mistake. "Quite a few people arbitrarily put friends and family off limits," he observes. "It's actually a professional move to begin a network with friends and family, because they know you well and will be some of your best advocates."

Another common mistake is to leave people off the list because they don't have a job to offer—for example, a friend who is currently unemployed. At this point you want to know people who know other people, especially those who have many acquaintances. A car service driver who makes twelve trips a day to the airport may be on friendly terms with many more managers than a corporate vice president! Your neighbor who works independently as a real estate agent may be the best connected person in town, even though she isn't hiring anyone, isn't in your industry, and doesn't work at a company. Never mind that they can't hire you—they can connect you, and that's what matters.

Consider as you list your comfort network not just whether you know someone, but whether they know you. This is an important difference, because early in your networking you want to contact people who are open to talking with you. They shouldn't be strangers, even if you know their names.

Bob Burg, author of *Endless Referrals,* suggests a system he calls "Yellow Pages and White Pages," and it's a great memory jogger. Try these two written exercises and see how many people you know.

EXERCISE 6

The "Yellow Pages" List

With a legal pad or computer at the ready, open a "yellow pages" phone directory. Go through the business categories from A to Z and list people you know in those professions. For example, starting with A: List everyone you know who's an actuary, an attorney, an accountant. B: List everyone you know who's a banker, a baker, a barber.

The key is to list people you know, not businesses you have heard about. These will be, for the most part, smaller businesses (that's the majority of listings); don't worry if they're not in your profession or if they aren't hiring. At this point, your goal is to create a list.

EXERCISE 7

The "White Pages" List

Now, turn to the "white pages" phone directory, and use the names in the directory to jog your memory. For example, who do you know named Abbott, Adams, or Allen? Who do you know named Barbara, Ben, or Bronson? Use first and last names for this exercise.

Of course, if you're using your hometown directory you'll see names of friends. Add them to your comfort network list.

Don't limit yourself to people in your geographic area—although you want to get face-to-face with people, strong contacts in distant locations can lead you back to further contacts nearby. As you make your list, don't get stalled thinking, "that person would never hear of a job." Remember: You do not know what, or who, other people know.

Very soon, you'll have a long list. In fact, you might be overwhelmed at the number of people you know! Soon you'll be talking to more people than you thought possible.

The First Calls

Now that you have a list of names, it's time to make some appointments. If you like, you can pick the most familiar name on the list for that first call—but treat the invitation to a networking conversation like you would a business appointment. Even if you're having coffee with your brother, actually call him and write a time on the calendar. Begin a contact file for him. Think in advance what you'll say (these early, friendly meetings are a great chance to refine your personal brand statement).

Janice Dilworth, an executive at Washington Mutual, advises networkers at this early stage to keep it simple: "To begin, you just start talking to people. You call people, you e-mail people, you meet them for coffee, and you ask them, 'Who do you know at ABC Company? May I contact them and use your name?'"

Starting with your comfort network allows you to put aside any image management issues you have about networking for a job. You're rehearsing for the more advanced meetings, which will come soon.

You can call up a friend and say, "Mary, you know I'm looking for a job and I've decided to get serious about networking. Could I meet with you to practice my networking conversation? I won't hit you up for a job but I'd like to find out what you know and who you know, and I also hope you'll listen to my little speech about who I am, what I do, and what I'm looking for. I'd like to practice my professional 'act' as well, so I'm going to dress up and ask if you'd meet me in your office or at a coffee shop in town."

If you actually make five appointments for the following week, you'll be on your way. Each meeting can result in referrals that lead to more meetings. Each meeting can give you confidence to go back to your comfort network list and set up more conversations. Thus, each meeting can bring you closer to that dream job.

Starting with your comfort network, you'll see that list of contacts growing quickly toward people who *do* know about a job opportunity. Your network will grow in unexpected directions, and soon it will contain more "professional contacts" than initial members of your familiar comfort network. A career network expands beyond the familiar bounds of your comfort network, and that's fine; you always have that comfort network to return to if you need it.

Serendipity will play a role for you, even in your early networking. Career networks grow in unanticipated directions because people's relationships grow and change and intersect in unpredictable ways. Your best friend's spouse's sister works at a company you target. Your neighbor's brother is a recruiter in your field. Your friend from the dog park spent two years working with someone you'd like to meet. You can't map these connections in advance, yet they will appear if you keep at your networking conversations.

Sarah Makes a Connection

Sarah looked at all the names on her comfort network list. They were a mixed bunch—colleagues, neighbors, friends, and relatives. There were even a few people she knew just a little—Kenny the plumber, and that nice woman in the library, Robin something. Even though she didn't remember Robin's last name, she felt comfortable with her. It must have been all those chats about books they were reading.

Only a few people on the list worked in Sarah's line of business, but she had to trust that they could lead her to job openings. Luis and Michelle had insisted that Sarah practice networking first with people she already knew, and explained that she would work her way toward a job from there.

Sarah noticed her friend Martin's name next to the number 48 on her list. Why hadn't she called him weeks ago? Probably because Martin was so quiet and introverted that he could be hard to remember.

Luis had told her, though, that someone's personal style shouldn't keep him out of her comfort network. The only qualification for getting on the list was trust—and Sarah trusted Martin. They had worked together on a brutally difficult project six years before, shutting down a failed product line, and she had seen his character in those trying last weeks. As the project manager of the shutdown (they had called her "Empress of the Dead"), Sarah saw many employees doing the least work they possibly could. Martin, however, had run the company's Web site until the last day, and spent hours on the phone to customers, a job he clearly disliked.

Now Martin was employed in another company, and they hadn't talked in two years, but Sarah was sure he'd be glad to hear from her. She wrote the letter A next to his name.

Sarah found Martin's e-mail address, then started to compose a message: "Hey there, Martin—it's Sarah, and it's been a while since we talked. My bad. I'd like to tell you what I'm doing today and ask for your help. . . ."

EXERCISE 8

First Networking List

If you've finished chapter 3 without starting that comfort network list, this is the time to do it! Make your list, choose five people to contact, and then create a contact file for each person you call. You'll quickly get into a habit that pays off in your job search and throughout your career! Here's a typical list of names and relationships, which is helpful for this first list. We'll revisit this growing list at the end of chapter 4.

1. Mary Gallagher (sister)

2. Larry Newman (from previous job)

3. Robert Warren (Larry's best friend)

4. Samantha Proctor (Girl Scout leader)

5. Cinny Green (neighbor—works at ABC Co.)

6. Ralph C. Pemberton (Cinny's boyfriend, offered to help)

4 Face-to-Face

This is the step you've anticipated with eagerness, dread—or both. You're going face-to-face. Even if your first meetings are with members of your comfort network, you might still feel nervous.

If you've done your homework so far, you can repeat a personal brand statement and talk about employers in which you're interested. You can tell stories that give people a clear idea of your "selling points" to an employer. You are prepared for a great conversation! You're ready to learn a process that moves smoothly into a strong networking routine.

I'll show you how to structure a networking meeting that gets results and still allows natural conversation. Do this five times with friends, and you can venture confidently outside your comfort network. At the end of every meeting, you'll add referral names to your network.

Soon after each meeting, you'll follow up with both contacts and referrals, and establish positive ways to stay in touch. You'll start to expand your career network list well beyond your initial comfort network, returning as appropriate to the initial list.

Now your networking leaves the abstract nature of a list and becomes more a series of give-and-take conversations.

Finally, you'll practice the more subjective task of making priorities among the people in your network. You'll learn to recognize (in this and subsequent chapters) which contacts bring you closer to your goals, and develop a habit of paying closer attention to them.

The Swan in His Nest

Martin had been working on a software code problem for five hours, and it looked like it was finally straightened out. He uploaded a patch to the test server and then notified the Quality Assurance team to test it out. Five hours of very intense code analysis. A good day.

He opened his e-mail and saw the message from Sarah. She was looking for work. Surprising, thought Martin . . . Sarah's really good in project management. I guess the job market's tough out there if she's having trouble.

Martin slid almost supine in his chair, hands on the keyboard, typing his reply:

Hi, Sarah:
Good to hear from you. I'd love to bring you in for an interview here but my boss just quit and we're not going to hire anyone until he's replaced. Anyway, I don't think you'd like it here.

Martin almost wrote, "especially since Pete left us such a honkin' big mess to clean up," then decided, well, that's kind of confidential. He thought a moment and continued,

I could introduce you to some friends. Bridget Conway at Challenge Corp. is really good. I'll follow this e-mail with another introducing you. By the way, while I'm roasting in hell

here, doing my job and my former boss's job too, what's it like
to be out there playing footsie with headhunters all day?
Yeah, I thought so. ☹
Hang in there,
Martin

The Flow of a Networking Meeting

The following six-item agenda for a networking meeting can be used
with people in your comfort network; it may seem a little extra businesslike in tone because you'll actually be rehearsing to meet with
strangers. (From now on, I'll refer to the person you're meeting as
your "contact," whether they are an old friend or a stranger.)

Propose a face-to-face meeting in a neutral setting like a workplace
conference room or a coffee shop. Avoid meeting at a private home
unless your contact is a good friend, because the distractions of a home
tend to dilute the professional focus of the conversation (home offices are a possible exception).

People who know you well may think it's a little strange to hold a
structured conversation. In most cases, they know you're looking for
a job. They think they can describe what you do. You need to practice
in front of a friendly audience, however, and they need to get your
version of your personal brand if they're going to be any help in
spreading the word.

At their best, networking meetings feel like a friendly conversation
and cover the important business topics—your personal brand, research, and referrals. Sometimes the conversation is extremely comfortable, but not always productive, and you have to remind yourself
of the goals.

Here's the model agenda for a networking meeting:

- Establish rapport.
- State your objective early (referrals or actual job leads).

- Pass along your personal brand statement (and with a friend, ask for feedback).
- Ask questions to research possible employers, jobs, and industry information.
- Make the exchange a two-way street by offering help.
- Get referrals.

Let's look at each step:

Establish Rapport.

Most networking conversations start with small talk, and for a good reason. Small talk establishes rapport, and without that, the conversation doesn't move along. Small talk also begins to establish common ground. Your chat about the community, the mutual friend who brought you together, or the café or office where you meet sets others at ease. It gives you a chance to display enthusiasm for the meeting, and provides openings for the business conversation. For example: "It was good of Evan to introduce us. He's an outstanding coach. I notice he never loses his temper, even when a kid is giving him a hard time. That must be a strength of his at work."

State Your Objective.

Early on, be clear that you are expanding your web of relationships to locate a job opportunity. All your contact needs to do is answer a few questions and think about their own relationships (or career network). Don't rush into a request for referrals until your contact has a very clear notion of who you are and what you're looking for.

Share Your Personal Brand.

Often your contact, trying to be helpful, will say, "Tell me about yourself." Quickly state the points of your personal brand. Don't stop at the job title, but repeat the entire personal brand statement you prepared in chapter 3. Help people understand the benefits of what you do in a business context; this helps them make great referrals. Depending on your relationship, you may want to conclude by asking, "Have I been really clear? Could you give a stranger a clear description of me?"

Ask Questions for Research and Referrals.

One of the easiest ways to focus the conversation on employment is to show a typed list of target employers and ask, "Do you know anyone I may speak to at any of these organizations?" Give your contact time to study the list. It helps if you group the employers on your list into categories like Manufacturing, Professional Services, Health Care, and so forth.

A list of real names is important to jog your contact's memory. Saying "a midsize consumer company" is vague. Saying "Oakley, Eddie Bauer, L.L. Bean, or similar companies," is specific. If they cannot think of anyone right away, ask if there are any firms you've missed that belong on the list. Often they will know someone at a company they suggest.

And listen. Listening is a vital component to career networking that too many people fail to master. Resist the urge to talk all about yourself. People like to be heard, and one simple way to make a good impression is to listen carefully. Listening is also research, especially when it comes to spotting job opportunities, potential employers, or well-connected individuals.

Listening and asking questions helps the common ground appear naturally. It's during the conversation that you find out the marketing guru you've wanted to meet shares your love of whitewater kayaking! Or, your contact says he's looking for a good place to get stationery printed, and you recommend a print shop you like. It's when the conversation flows like this that the "small world" connections appear.

Although your contact might want to be helpful, he or she may be unsure how to help. You can "help them help you" by asking questions that lead you to a better understanding of their work. Questions revive a lagging conversation, and lead the conversation naturally toward referrals. Try to learn what they do, why they like doing it, and who else they know, with questions such as:

- Tell me about your job; why did you choose this career?
- Tell me about your employer's business.
- Who do you work for?

- Who works for you—what are their skills, and what makes them successful?
- Who are your customers? Where are they located?
- Who is your competition and where is it located?
- Which companies/organizations do you most respect in this business?
- Which employers in this area really impress you?
- If you were to move on to another position, what would it be?
- Who else does a job like yours?
- What employers are growing now in this business?
- If I were to say I'm looking for this job (describe), who do you know who could tell me more?
- That's an interesting problem; how did you solve it?
- What's the best thing about your current employer?
- What's your biggest challenge today?
- Why did you decide to create that product?
- Who else should I meet?
- If I could take just one piece of advice from you about [this business, my job search, etc.] what would it be?
- We haven't yet spoken about [topic]. May I ask you some questions about that?

You should have at least ten questions to draw on as your reliable conversation helpers, but you don't have to overstructure the conversation. If you ask all these questions one after another, you're going to sound more like a reporter than someone expanding their network. Be alert to interesting new subjects you might explore, such as your contact's casual mention of a tiny start-up company you hadn't heard of before. Often people you meet will close the meeting by asking you if you have any questions, and even though this is a cue to wrap things up, always save one or two short questions for then if you can. It's better to finish a meeting with a few small questions unanswered than to run out of questions.

Try This

Questions

Before any networking meeting, write down five general questions that interest you (you can pick them from the list above) and five specific questions, based on what you know about your contact, their employer, or industry, such as:

- I studied your Web site, and I'd like to know more about the following issues: [name them].
- Bob told me you were responsible for opening up the Asian markets for your company's product. How are you doing that?
- I hear you also participate in the "Run for a Cure" event. Can you tell me more about that organization?
- What happened with the online/offline partnership your company announced a year ago? How's that going?

If you don't have enough information to come up with five specific questions, you need to dig a little deeper—go back to the person who referred you to the contact, or to Internet research, and get more! (Do this even if the meeting is an informational interview; see page 62.)

Offer to Help.

When you find out more about a contact, you can imagine ways in which you can be helpful to them. Learn to ask, "What can I do for you?" If you have listened well, you should be able to ask this in a more specific way. If your contact can't think of ways you can help them, offer to make introductions, which is exactly what you hope your contact will do for you:

- May I introduce you to someone who may be helpful to you?
- You're interested in finding new print vendors. A friend I know has used several. Would you like to talk to her?
- When you mentioned you are looking for a tutor for your daughter, I immediately thought of a friend whose wife is a

math tutor. I hear she's very good. Would you like me to introduce her to you?

These introductions are made for specific reasons, not just because you know someone. Always offer to make the introduction personally—this is another way for you to follow up, reconnect, and reinforce your broad relationship-building skills.

If you have no introduction to make, you can still offer help throughout the conversation, for example:

- I just saved a great newsletter article on that subject, and I'll send it to you.
- We just set up a wireless network at home using a how-to guide I got online. Let me e-mail that to you, since you want to do it, too. And if you have any questions, feel free to ask.
- If you're responsible for setting up a mailing list for the Community Chest, I can show you how to do that.

However the conversation flows, your networking contact is approaching a decision as the conversation closes: How willing am I to give him or her my best referrals? This is the heart of the relationship you've been building for the previous hour. They will be protective of their relationships, so while you may request a referral, do not pursue it if they decline. If you continue a good networking relationship over time, they'll remember that you really want to meet the CEO of their company.

The rule to follow: Be a little more helpful than you're asking someone else to be.

But, having said that, don't bite off more than you can chew. If you commit to a thousand favors in a week, you won't have time to look for a job or do the job you have! An introduction takes ten minutes to make via e-mail. "Keeping your eyes open" for another person in this way is exactly what you'll hope they do for you. On the other hand, committing to volunteer for someone else's favorite charitable cause is probably too time-consuming. Keep your offer open, but manage your commitments wisely.

Sometimes a contact will decline your help. Perhaps they perceive such an imbalance in status or information that they're just doing you a favor. (This typically happens when an executive gives an informational interview to a new graduate.) Remember that you are giving them a chance to be helpful, which makes them feel good. If your contact declines, don't beat the offer to death.

Even if your early contacts are close friends in your comfort network, you should practice this step, because simply doing it will alert you to new ways you can be helpful.

Refocus on Referrals at the End.

The end of the meeting is your final opportunity to request referrals if they have not yet been offered. If your contact is willing but unable to think of someone, you can suggest:

- Anyone connected with an employer you mentioned.
- Anyone who might work with them.
- Anyone who might benefit from a conversation with you.
- Anyone who is well connected in general.

When asking questions, be alert to the fact that they might be thinking in a box. A typical response is, "Hey, I'd love to help you find architectural work, but I don't know any architects." You are not demanding that your contact know of a job opening for an architect—you're asking them who they know who might be connected with an architect in any way.

Bear in mind the inter-related nature of businesses. When an architect, realtor, mortgage originator, banker, town planner, closing attorney, and home inspector get in a room, they can't help but pass business back and forth because their work is all concerned with people buying homes. They have the same clients but they're not competing, which is a natural reason for a cooperative partnership. Who are the natural partners in your profession?

This is a good time to return to the list of potential employers, and ask:

- Do you still think these are the right employers for me?
- Can you think of potential employers who are not on this list?
- Are there people we've mentioned who you would be willing to refer me to?

After you've got some names down, review the referrals with them: "Okay, you have an idea of the message I'd like to send out there, and you know the following people: [list them]. Shall I contact them or do you want to make the referral?"

It is much more effective for your contact to make the referral personally. First, request that they make the introduction themselves. The best introduction begins, "Mary, I want you to meet a friend of mine named Bob Smith. Bob's working in your field and I think you'd be interested to meet him."

Ask your contact to notify you when they make that introduction (and follow up if it slips their mind). Commonly, your contact will send an e-mail introduction, copying you and the new contact; you take it from there.

Of course, you can't push them to introduce you personally, so if they insist, "You just get in touch and mention my name," you're still in business.

The Agenda and Your Style

The six-item agenda I've just described doesn't change according to your networking style. Whether you're a swan, butterfly, dolphin, or lion, you have to establish rapport, ask questions, and get referrals. What does change is your comfort level at various points in the conversation, and the things you are prone to overlook. So here's a guide to stepping outside your comfort zone for the sake of effectiveness:

Swan-style networkers feel as if they've done enough just getting to the meeting. You've probably been diligent about your homework, so don't be shy about showing that off. Ask deep questions that show off your research. If expressing a personal brand with an "elevator speech" is just excruciating, you can place a written version in front of your contact and ask, "Does this give you a clear idea of who I am and what I do?"

Butterfly networkers love to meet people and love to talk; my suggestion is that you slow down a little the night before your meeting, review the chapter up to this point, and really prepare your questions. Write them down. And after the meeting, don't forget to follow up (see page 58).

Dolphin-style networkers should remember to put the focus on the contact and make sure *they're* feeling comfortable. Do they really want to be part of your network? Can you connect them to someone valuable? Tell your contact that you'll be following up, but don't scare them away.

Lion-style networkers are very comfortable in this one-to-one situation, so much so that, if their contact is more of a swan or a dolphin, the contact can feel intimidated. Don't solve all the problems of the world in one sitting. Don't ask fifty questions when three will suffice. Lions make a strong first impression, and make their contacts feel like the object of all their attention (because for one hour, they are).

Contacting Referrals

You have practiced the six-item agenda several times with low-risk people, and you have your first referrals. Now, you have to talk to a stranger. It's time to meet with someone who doesn't know you beyond that referral.

If your friend declines to make the introduction personally, the introduction is a little less forceful, but it doesn't change your approach to the next step, a step that causes more stumbles than others: Get in touch with those referrals right away! Within twenty-four hours, call or e-mail them with a simple statement like, "My name is Bob Smith, and my friend Janet Jones suggested we talk because I'm an electrical engineer, and I am talking to people in companies like yours. . . ."

Now the question will inevitably come up again: "Are you looking for work?" If you make that the focus of the initial contact, you risk cutting off the conversation before it starts (they'll think, "Well, I'm not hiring, so there's no reason to meet"). Focus on the conversation you want to have. You are not going to ask them for a job; you are going to ask for information. Most referrals respond positively to this; people really do want to help.

Conclude your message with that in mind: "I will eventually be looking for opportunities to bring my talents to a new employer, but for now I only want to find out more about your company, its products and business, its competitors and related companies. I want to introduce myself in case you know someone else I should meet. Janet said you'd be well informed and thought you might be available to meet with me for twenty minutes."

They may ask for a resume. Matt Bud, chairman of The Financial Executives Networking Group (FENG), suggests you handle this request simply. "They know why you're calling, so first send them a resume with a brief cover note telling them about yourself. I like to say that speech is the slowest form of communication, and if you have to explain your background that's five minutes of your phone call."

In other words, if they want to be all business, follow their lead. If they like what they see, they'll think of you when a job opening or business opportunity appears. They'll make referrals.

Some people will put you off, or won't respond to your e-mail or calls. Don't take it personally. People are very busy, they're afraid they won't be able to help you, they think their job's in jeopardy—a hundred reasons. Keep in touch once a month and they'll respond when they can.

But most people will reply because they have a stake in the referral. Patti Salvucci of BNI gives this example: "I once contacted a friend asking for twenty minutes to locate some people who might be interested in a breakfast networking program. When I asked, 'Who's the best printer in town, who's the best electrician?' she pulled some cards from her Rolodex. I called each person and I said, 'You don't know me but you were highly recommended by my friend Joan of the Civic League,' and they replied, 'Oh I've known Joan for 20 years! How can I help you?' The rapport was already established."

All Patti had to do was ask, and that's your job, too. Congratulations—your network is already expanding!

Networking with a Referral

I hope that practice with people in your comfort network has given you confidence. Now that you've arranged to meet with the referrals you've gotten from your first round of networking, you have to prepare more thoroughly. You get only one chance to make a first impression on a new contact.

If you are meeting with an individual via a referral, ask the person who referred you about them. Research them and their company in the library or online. At the least, you should know what they do for a living, where they fit into their organization, what they are trying to accomplish, and if they know anyone else in your network. If the person has been quoted in a news story or book, or if their biography appears on a Web site, you can make that a talking point for your conversation.

Review your own list of contacts before going. Since one of the most valuable things you can offer is connections, you want to have those fresh in your mind for the moment when a networking contact asks, "Hey, do you know anyone who. . . ." Then you can say, "Yes, you have to talk to my friend Jane. She can be very helpful for this. Give me your card and I will make an introduction."

Bring your networking kit along, but leave your resume in your briefcase unless it's requested.

Always arrive on time or a few minutes early. Dress appropriately. If you're meeting on a workday, that means a suit or jacket and tie for men, and a suit or skirt and blazer for women. At a more casual time, you might dress in a business-casual style, but don't show up in worn jeans and your favorite Jimmy Buffett T-shirt.

Shake hands firmly. Smile warmly. Your demeanor affects the conversation as much as your words. Are you interesting? Enthusiastic? Confident?

If you are handed a business card early in the conversation, don't immediately put it away but study it for a moment. What's the name of the contact's company? Where are they located? Is the card elaborately designed? There are good conversation cues there.

As the conversation gets under way, your body language conveys much of your message. For example, sitting up straight and leaning forward slightly indicates interest, eagerness, and energy—all good messages that say "You're interesting; I value what you say." Leaning back or slumping in your chair sends the opposite message. If you fidget, or frequently lose eye contact, you might appear nervous or evasive.

Your facial expression signals your attitude, especially when you listen. Look people in the eye and acknowledge their comments. In American business culture, roving eyes are a conversation killer; you might as well say, "I'm not really interested in you, I'm looking for something better." Standing or sitting close to someone can break down mental barriers (like being intimidated by a potential employer), but if you lean too close, your contact may interpret that as inappropriate or "pushy."

Just as in a job interview, differences in personal style can come into play, and they can be subtle. To some, long eye contact establishes trust; to others, it's intimidating. Sometimes you'll want to maintain a formal presence, sitting across a desk, and at other times a casual setting is more appropriate. For example, I give informational interviews in my office sitting in overstuffed leather chairs, with no desk, and the casual atmosphere sets people at ease.

"Thanks, and I'll Follow Up"

You'll say "thank you" at the end of the conversation. If you haven't done so yet, exchange business cards, or confirm contact information for referrals. Either way, promise that you'll stay in touch. As soon as the meeting is over, write notes into your contact system, paying special attention to however you promised to follow up (that goes on your calendar). Don't trust your memory! When you have 300 names in your contact list, you'll be glad you developed the note-taking habit early in this process.

Your next step—as soon as you get home—is to begin your follow-up.

Within **twenty-four hours** of a networking meeting, send a thank-you note. Personalized note cards are best for this, because they imply a closer relationship than "just doing business." Expert networkers use cards that are funny, or dramatic, or beautifully designed; these are memorable. Include your contact information on the envelope and on the card.

Today, people wonder if an e-mail or handwritten follow-up message is more appropriate. Actually, the two forms serve different purposes, and you should use both. E-mail doesn't replace a handwritten note, but it is an important part of your follow-up strategy. Send an e-mail within two days. Write a compelling subject line for the e-mail so your message doesn't get lost among 300 unread messages. For example: "Here's the address of that tax accountant we discussed," or "You mentioned a company in Rochester. . . ." You can finish a subject line like this at the top of the message: ". . . but you couldn't remember the name—is it ABC Co.?" These e-mail subject lines contain a call to action, and you want the recipient to take action on your behalf. Say thanks in the body of the message, reiterate your offer to help them, and politely remind your contact of a commitment they made such as getting you contact information for a referral or finding the title of that book they recommended.

J. Scott Hoyland, of video production company DigiNovations, has for years used networking to land customers. He believes in multiple follow-up and offers this sequence: "First, I send them an e-mail with information I've promised. As soon as the e-mail is sent, I call and tell them everything that was in the e-mail. If they don't pick up, I leave a detailed voice mail: I'll say, 'I met you last night, here's my name, I just sent you the information I promised in an e-mail with the following title. . . .' I leave the voice mail for two reasons: it's easier to listen to a phone message than read an e-mail, and I don't want my e-mail to be mistaken for spam."

At this point, many job seekers drop their communication. They think either their contact has nothing more to offer, or that they will become a pest. They got the referral, so why annoy a contact with regular e-mails?

Because you're conducting a relationship, that's why. Strong networking relationships are open-ended; the referral is just the next step. If you drop out of sight, your busy contact will move on and the relationship will languish. But if you drop a line to let the contact know how the meeting went with the referral and thanking them again, or referring them to someone you've met, not only are you reinserting yourself into the person's consciousness, but you're building the foundation of a meaningful, straightforward, symbiotic relationship that benefits both parties.

Following up is also one of those acts of confidence that move networking forward. You might not know what's in it for you . . . today. Perhaps you'll get a payoff next week, or two years from now, or never. Often, the payoff comes in a completely unexpected form. You cannot predict what will happen; you can only set the process in motion.

You must follow up on referrals *both* ways—contact the referral *and* tell your original contact that you've followed up. Dr. Ivan Misner of BNI says this is the top habit of successful networkers. It expands your network, of course, but more important, it fulfills a commitment you made to the original contact. They know you do what you say. If you contact referrals right away, and they agree to talk to you, that's another opportunity to touch base with the person who connected you. The relationship continues.

How you follow up depends on the contact's priority in your career network. If they're providing meaningful referrals, keep in touch every couple of weeks with an e-mail. Find a specific reason: "I read that ABC Company is revamping its main product line and remembered you used to work there. Is there anyone there, an old colleague of yours perhaps, who could tell me more about this?"

As time passes, it's important to establish an update routine. You have to remind people that you exist (especially if you're still looking for a job). The need for repetition is basic to networking: people get busy and fall out of touch—and you retreat further from their minds.

Here are professional ways to get back in touch after some time has passed:

- Send a progress report. Keep it brief and high-level, and reiterate your message: "I've had some great conversations, and discovered some interesting developments in our industry. I'm always looking for new relationships, so please pass my name along to anyone you think might be interested in a conversation."

- Send another article or news item that is relevant to their business. If you found the information online, send the article as an attachment or a Web link.
- Send a personal message describing how the recipient's referral led to another referral, and another. People love to hear that their conversation led eventually to eight or ten additional conversations (and you'll get a reputation as a serious networker).

People with very large personal networks sometimes send a regular e-mail newsletter or keep a less formal Internet "listserv" communication open. This method has a place in long-term business networking, but when you're looking for work you should communicate in a more personal way.

When you do land a job, drop a note to everyone you spoke to, no matter how insignificant their contribution, just to thank them for being part of your process. No one minds being thanked, and this professional courtesy sets you apart, just because it's so rarely done.

Sarah Adds Another Person to Her Network

"Are you Sarah?" asked the woman at the corner table.

"Yes, and you must be Martin's friend Bridget," said Sarah. She set her coffee on the table and extended her hand. "It's good of you to see me."

Bridget motioned for Sarah to sit, and said, "Martin spoke very highly of you. Or I should say, he *wrote* very highly of you. I don't think I've actually spoken to the man in six months, even though we e-mail each other all the time."

Sarah smiled ruefully. "Martin hasn't changed. I remember when we worked together at Challenge Corporation, that he would rather send an instant message than walk thirty feet for a face-to-face conversation."

They talked for a few minutes about the Challenge Corporation, whose demise had cost Sarah her last job. Then Bridget said crisply,

"Martin told me you'd like to know more about my company. I should mention up front that we're not hiring anyone in your field right now."

"That's fine," said Sarah. "Because while I'd love to hear about a job opening, I'm more interested at this point in just talking to as many people as I can about their work."

Bridget visibly relaxed. "Oh, well, that's easy!" she said. "What can I tell you?"

"Let's start with what you do," said Sarah.

They talked for an hour, until Bridget said, "I have to go in a few minutes, but I feel as if all I've done is talk about myself. What can I do for you?"

"You've already done a lot," said Sarah. She pointed to her small notepad. "I've got the names of three companies I never knew about, and several people you've mentioned. You know a little bit about who I am, where I've worked, and what I do, so let me ask you—are there people you can think of that you would be comfortable introducing me to, for a conversation just like this?"

"Oh, of course!" replied Bridget. She pointed to the notepad as well. "You can get in touch with Wayne Conway there, and with George Bass, that consultant I told you about."

"Great!" said Sarah.

"On second thought," continued Bridget, "let me introduce you personally to George. I owe him a call anyway, and you'll do better if I recommend you."

Sarah nodded. "Thanks, that's really good of you. You've already given me a lot of your time. Now, what can I do for you?"

Informational Interviews

The informational interview is different from the networking meeting in that its initial focus is to research a job, company, or industry you're considering. Briefly, in an informational interview you ask someone about his or her job, company, industry, and overall career.

It becomes part of your career networking when the person refers you to someone they know who may lead you closer to a job. Now it's not just research—the interview has morphed into a networking meeting.

The ideal genesis of an informational interview is a referral from someone in your network, but you can also approach anyone directly for an informational interview as part of a job search—first e-mail them and call to set an appointment. I think you should mention networking in your request: "I'm hoping to find out more about your business, and I'm also expanding my network of contacts as part of my job search." People grant informational interviews as a favor to you, and they should know what to expect (which is, you'll eventually ask them for referrals).[2]

This is a natural setting for networking. You're not pressuring someone for a particular job, and the person has already consented to help. The questions you ask can be similar to the questions listed above, with generally more emphasis on the particular business and field of expertise of the interviewee and his or her employer. When you realize that an informational interview has evolved into a networking meeting, don't be shy about asking for referrals.

Although we usually think of these conversations as serving only the person looking for a job, I believe there can be a lot in it for the person granting the interview. I do a lot of informational interviews and notice which people keep in touch after the interview. If they actively keep in touch, I'm more likely to think of them when a friend asks if I know anyone with their skills who's looking for a job. When they land in another company, I still remember them. Our paths may cross a few years down the line.

If you're currently in a job, one of the best ways to network is to solicit informational interviews. When you hear about someone who's looking say, "Come on in, let me tell you about my company." Do that once a month and you'll have twelve grateful new people in your career network by next year—people who eventually land in a job and have the energy to stay in touch.

[2] To learn more about informational interviews, see *Monster Careers: How to Land the Job of Your Life*, pp. 246–250.

Make Priorities

As your career network grows through referrals, you'll discover that you have more names than you could possibly talk to in a week, a month, or even a year. This is a good problem to have! You solve it by making priorities.

Start simply, but methodically. On your contact file, put the letter A in the "Priority" box next to the best connections in your network. These are people who have one or more of the following:

- Can describe you in business terms (your personal brand).
- Will act as your advocate with enthusiastic referrals.
- Are well connected and active (the "connectors" mentioned earlier).
- Work for employers who interest you.

Write the letter B on the contact files of people who don't necessarily have the ability, or willingness, to help. Here are some examples of B-level contacts:

- Someone who is well connected but doesn't feel comfortable recommending you.
- Someone who knows you well but just can't think of a referral.
- Someone you don't feel quite comfortable about (but may someday—for example, a well-connected former boss or one of your nutty in-laws).

Keep a record of B-level contacts for those times when you've talked to all the As on your list. As you grow in confidence, you may decide that a B-level contact can become an A with a little extra work on your part.

One simple way to work with Bs is to notify them that you're looking for job connections. Drop them an occasional e-mail just to keep yourself from slipping off the radar.

I've noticed that there are a few C-level contacts in everyone's network. They're just potential A or B contacts, and probably can't (or won't) network actively, but for various reasons you just can't cross their name off your contact list. Go ahead and leave them on the list. Some of them will probably come up in your networking conversations, and you don't want to forget them entirely.

Adjust your contact files as you go. Some people who you think today are As may work their way down to Cs, says Diane Darling, CEO of Effective Networking. "The number one way to bounce down the list is if they do not return your phone call," she says. "Keep prioritizing your network—their behavior tells you how much they value you."

As you assign priority to contacts, bear in mind the limitations that some people face in making referrals. Your local golf pro may know a lot of high-powered executives but feels obligated to protect their privacy. A doctor or attorney may make some referrals and withhold others. An executive friend from the soccer field may simply have a "no referrals" policy until he knows you better.

Momentum

Networking guru Dr. Ivan Misner likes to remind people that "it's net-*work*, not net-sit or net-eat."

This is detective work. You'll pick up clues here and there—names of people, potential target companies, and ideas for new connections. Once the momentum is going, the network almost propagates itself. Soon, your expanding web of relationships will influence other parts of your job search. Commonly, a network conversation will add new names to your list of target companies. Even more significantly, your networking conversations may alter the direction of your search by revealing new ways you may use your skills.

Most important, don't break your momentum waiting for a response. Never hang by the phone, hoping someone will call. When nobody's calling, get in touch with five more people. One or more of them will say "yes" and lead you to more referrals.

EXERCISE 9

Expanded Networking List

Return to the sample network list shown on page 43. You've contacted each of the people on the list, and actually had a networking face-to-face with four of them. Three made referrals. Now, expand the list to show how your career network has grown. Here's an example based on the previous sample list (note that each connection also has been assigned a priority level). In this example, the list of six has expanded to fifteen in one round of networking.

1. Mary Gallagher (sister) **Priority** $\boxed{A}$
    a. Alex Olsen (works with Mary)
    b. Donna Sawyer (Mary's customer)
    c. Pete Rice (Mary's friend)
2. Larry Newman (from previous job) **Priority** $\boxed{A}$
    a. Sylvia Duarte (friend of Larry's—works at ABC Co.)
    b. Deborah Guilmette
3. Robert Warren (Larry's best friend) **Priority** $\boxed{C}$ (said on the phone he doesn't want to meet but "ask me later")
4. Samantha Proctor (Girl Scout leader) **Priority** $\boxed{B}$ (good talk but didn't have referrals)
5. Cinny Green (neighbor—works at ABC Co.) **Priority** $\boxed{A}$
    a. Lori Castillo (head of HR at ABC Co.)
    b. Nat Ramsey (friendly ex-husband; manager at XYZ Inc.)
    c. John Bartlett (Runs sales dept at 123 Co.)
    d. Nichole Stein (Recruiter—got Cinny into ABC Co.)
6. Ralph C. Pemberton (Cinny's boyfriend, offered to help) **Priority** $\boxed{B}$ (trading e-mail messages—promising but haven't yet met him)

Now, as a preview of where you can go with this, let's take just one of those initial six connections and map out three rounds of networking and referrals:

1. Mary Gallagher (sister) **Priority** [A]
   a. Alex Olsen (works with Mary)
      i. Bart Thomas
         1. Walter Thomas
         2. Anne Newman
      ii. Will Shenker
         1. Abby Rubin
   b. Donna Sawyer (Mary's customer)
      i. Jean Callaway
      ii. Mark Rogers
         1. Keith Campbell
   c. Pete Rice (Mary's friend)
      i. Meredith Stanhope
         1. Rachel Stanhope
         2. Mary Ng
         3. Michael DeWolfe
      ii. Charlie Halloway

The first person on your list has led to sixteen connections in just three steps! How many connections could you make from, say, an initial comfort network list of twenty—even including the B- and C-priority people?

A lot, that's how many. Can you see how quickly a network expands? Can you imagine how quickly you'll be talking to people who know about your dream job?

In fact, it's soon cumbersome to actually make a list in this format. You'll have to rely on individual contact records to keep it organized. The illustrations above are meant to help you envision your growing career network. In real practice, the expansion of your career network will be like other human processes—it will grow in unexpected directions, some people will drop out of sight, and sometimes serendipity will lead you to a great connection. A career network grows in many directions at once, organically and unpredictably. You don't have to overanalyze it—just keep putting energy into it.

Closing In on a Job

As you expand your network, you'll hit an important milestone: actually talking to someone who works at a potential employer. In this case, you might shift the objective of your conversation from gaining more referrals to getting a first shot at a job opening. You're also looking to see if they'll put in a good word. Ask more directed questions about the company. Who do they know in a department where you might work? What is the company culture like, and where are the opportunities emerging? If you build a good relationship with an insider, they'll refer you to the hiring manager before that job even becomes public knowledge. Keep in mind: Companies often reward current employees for successful referrals handsomely. If you make the right impression, this meeting could benefit both of you.

The other benefit of networking conversations and informational interviews within target companies is that they are much less pressured than job interviews. You can find out a lot about what the organization seeks in its employees without the cold sweats and stage fright that all job interviews seem to inspire. After all, you're just having a conversation. Even if that conversation may evolve into a job interview down the line, the pressure, for the moment, is off. Take advantage of this. Be yourself. Treat these insiders to the same help you would offer anyone. It's easy to imagine that you have little to offer someone in a position of power at a target company, but that's selling yourself short. At the very least, you can offer referrals from your network, and often you'll find that they are interested in the perspective that your networking has given you. Most managers know they should network, but they never seem to have time for it.

The dream scenario unfolds when a contact refers you to someone who can create a job for you. If you make the right impression—if you're informed, well-spoken, and well-connected (as your networking can make you) and if you share those benefits generously—they will start to imagine you on their team. They'll think, "This is a very impressive person; I wonder where they might fit in this company?" Sometimes I've seen these informal relationships bypass the formal job interview process!

Now that you've begun growing a career network with face-to-face conversations, and you've got some real practice in place, you're going to take it one step further. You're going to cast an even wider net and go into large-group settings. Walking into a room of people with the intention of making new relationships is the next test of the career networker . . . and a heck of a lot of fun, too.

5 In a Crowded Room

When you go to a networking event, your objective is to make the **best** possible connections with the **most** possible people in the **shortest** amount of time. Sometimes you'll meet interns and sometimes you'll end up talking with the very person who can hire you tomorrow. Often you'll run into independent people who aren't looking for a job but are there to learn something new, or to find a new customer. Every one of them is there to engage—what better place to build all kinds of professional relationships than at events that are dedicated to networking?

Martin Makes a Connection

"I never should have let you talk me into this," said Martin.

"Relax, Martin. This is good for you," said Sarah.

"Nuts. I have got to get out of here."

Sarah did not stop scanning the ballroom that she had just maneuvered—no, *dragged*—Martin across. "Relax," she repeated. "Just one new person, that's all. Then you can go home." Sarah had seen Michelle engaged in an intense discussion with three men who clearly seemed to know her. Clients, probably.

"We're going to find you a good connection," said Sarah.

"I don't need a good connection, I need a new boss," said Martin. "I'm totally swamped trying to do my job and taking care of all the fires my last boss left burning."

"Any chance they'll promote you into the job?" asked Sarah.

"Oh, please, not that," Martin moaned. "Senior managers get all the crap work and don't get any of the interesting work. I'm an engineer. I want to build great software, not figure out who's supposed to be head of the office-decorating committee."

"Just one person, then you can go," repeated Sarah, smiling.

"You introduce me to somebody," said Martin. Sarah felt his gaze on her. She had persuaded Martin to come to the monthly meeting of the Beltway Networkers in the conversations following her e-mail. Martin was happy enough in his current situation, but he had told her quietly that he was looking for a higher-paying job with more autonomy. He wanted to keep his search quiet during the shake-up at his company.

Sarah had noticed Luis right away, and had crossed the room intending to introduce him to Martin, but something had made her hesitate. She wanted to watch how the man Michelle described as an expert networker operated in a room full of strangers. Now, even though she couldn't hear his conversation, she could see Luis going through a deliberate kind of choreography: Luis stepped back from a group of four and gestured for a woman who was waiting at the periphery to join the group. Sarah hadn't even noticed her. Luis asked the new person a question, then appeared to introduce her to the group. Then he redirected attention back to the person who had been speaking. A few minutes later, he excused himself and walked purposefully toward another group, looking up and smiling cheerfully. Sarah saw him jot a note on a business card as he walked.

"Oh hey, Ben!" she exclaimed, waving to a large man in a polo shirt and blazer. She signaled him over, and as he approached, Sarah murmured to Martin, "Ben got laid off just before I did. He's a tech guy, too. Last I knew he was chief technology officer of a start-up. Come on and say hello." Martin's pained expression twisted into a grimace as Sarah greeted Ben.

"Ben, this is Martin," said Sarah. "Ben worked with me and we were both victims of the layoffs. You two both work on enterprise-level projects, so I thought you ought to meet." Martin and Ben shook hands, but said little. Sarah, alert to both men's discomfort, said, "Ben, I worked with Martin a couple of years ago; he's at Axis Partners now and I thought you two might have gone to the same school."

"Where'd you go?" Ben asked Martin.

"RPI," said Martin.

Brightening, Ben said, "Me, too. What year?" The men began to talk more easily.

Okay, thought Sarah, Martin's got his one contact. She scanned the room. Who else should I talk to tonight?

While you might be prepared for networking at any time, you have to show up in the right places deliberately. Woody Allen's observation that "80 percent of success in life is just showing up" is a central fact of career networking. A variety of professional venues provide opportunity, including focused business networking events, conferences in your profession or industry, workshops and seminars, trade shows, company parties, and virtually any other event where people gather to do business.

Network from Beginning to End

Let's set the scene for a networking event: You've decided to attend the monthly meeting of an organization in your industry. There will be a speaker, some discussion of a current issue in your business, and an hour devoted to networking. You'll be in a room with fifty to a hundred others.

Arrive on time or even a little early—this gives you a natural excuse to talk to the few people there. If someone's setting out chairs or arranging items on a reading table, go help them and strike up a conversation. At the door, when you're getting your name tag, talk to the person at the entryway—they usually work for the host, and can introduce you. "Thank you for hosting this event" is a good icebreaker, and your host might be the best-connected person in the room. Write your name in large block letters on your tag, and wear it below your right shoulder, so people can easily read it while shaking your hand. If you've set yourself the completely achievable goal of meeting one or two new people, you can tell yourself you've already achieved that goal (but stay anyway and keep it up!).

If you arrive alone, don't automatically head straight for the bathroom, which is pushing you away from the network. Look over the room and set a destination for yourself. Walk toward the breakfast table or the bar right away. You don't have to reach it—just use that walk to look around. Can you spot someone you know? Do you see a target company on a name tag? Be prepared to stop and introduce yourself. If someone is standing alongside, shake hands and suggest, "Let's get something at the bar," and keep moving. If you get stopped by someone you don't want to talk to right then, say, "Hi, I just got here, and I'll catch you later."

It's tempting to gravitate toward people you already know. That's your comfort zone; but you are there to develop new relationships, so fight the urge. That's the most common mistake I see when coworkers attend an event together: Three people from ABC Corp. walk into a networking meeting, and guess who they talk to while they're having drinks—each other. Guess who they sit with at dinner—each other. They accidentally meet somebody else at the table, but don't bring him or her into the conversation. Then they leave together and say, "Hey, that was a great networking event!"

No, it wasn't. None of them met a new person, or ventured out of his or her comfort zone.

If you go to an event with colleagues, split like an atom at the door. Go in different directions. Touch base halfway through the event; if someone's made an interesting connection, he should introduce his colleagues: "Bill, I'd like you to meet Stacey, who works at ABC Co. Stacey's an incredible organizer of the big-client sales cycle and I know she'd be interested to know about your work."

If you're unemployed, and run into a friend, they'll understand that you are there to meet new people. Propose that you team up: go in different directions for twenty minutes, and if either makes a connection that seems useful for the other, plan to introduce each other.

As you scan the room, think about who's at the event, and why they are there. Vendors and business owners go to a lot of these events prospecting for clients. They may have information that's useful to you, but be cautious of spending too much time listening to their sales pitch if you're keeping your focus on looking for job referrals.

Try This

Monster senior sales executive Carol McCarthy gave memorable advice to sales representatives attending a networking event: "Don't talk to anyone from work until you've met ten people you don't know. When you have collected ten new business cards, then you can talk to someone else from Monster."

Can you be as disciplined?

Get Into Groups

As you walk around, you'll notice lots of groups of three to six people. Did you decide in advance there's someone you want to meet? The high-interest person always has a group around him or her, so you'll probably have to break into an existing group. Many times you can join groups that are larger than four just by being in the area. In many ways it's not unlike dancing. People dance in groups and people dance as couples. When the time seems right, you can try to couple off into a conversation—sometimes it works and sometimes it doesn't; don't be frustrated by that, but move on to the next one.

Lots of potentially great connections get cut off at this first moment, when people fail to join a group. If you find it easy to walk right in, go for it. For the other 90 percent of you, here are some helpers suggested in a conversation with Susan RoAne, author of *How to Create Your Own Luck:*

- Body language counts for a lot. A closed circle of backs is uninviting at best. If you find yourself standing outside such a group, don't look down, but look directly into someone's eyes. Often, someone will stand back and bring you in.
- If nobody brings you in, find a lull in the conversation and step forward. This may be the time when simplest is best, so ask, "Excuse me, may I join you?"
- Double up—two people can join a group more comfortably than one.
- If you notice someone wants to join a group you're in, step back, turn toward them, and invite them to join. The person you invite may be the most interesting person you meet (and they'll remember your courtesy).

The Lion Hits a Wall

Michelle waved to Sarah and Martin, who stood talking to a large man in a polo shirt and blazer. She didn't joint them; it was time to get down to serious client hunting. She had come to the Beltway networkers event to introduce herself to Sean Jordan, the VP of sales at Chestnut Systems, and now she saw him, talking to a small group 20 feet away. Two people in Michelle's network had shared rumors that Chestnut's sales team was about to grow very quickly, and that made Jordan a great prospect for her sales-training business.

Michelle had not yet found a referral to introduce her to Jordan, but she didn't want to let this chance slip away. She moved into full Lion-networker mode, approaching the group where he stood, actually positioning herself so that, when she entered the circle, she would be directly across from Jordan. A woman in the group saw her and moved aside, inviting her to join. Michelle smiled her thanks and stepped into the circle.

Michelle could see from the group's behavior that Sean Jordan was the focus of everyone there. A stylishly dressed man to her left tried to question him several times, clearing his throat and interrupting the discussion Jordan held with another man.

When Jordan glanced briefly at Michelle and the man to her left, the rest of the group imitated the behavior. Michelle held her hand out to him, saying "Mr. Jordan, it's a pleasure to meet you, I'm Michelle. . . ."

The stylishly dressed man grabbed Jordan's hand and pumped it. "And I'm Hank Lyle, Sean. I called you a few times last week to talk about your sales group. . . ."

Jordan shook Lyle's hand quickly, and nodded at Michelle. Then he turned his back on both of them. He put his arm on another man's shoulder and said, "Let's find someplace quieter to talk." Without turning to acknowledge the group, the two men walked away.

Okay, thought Michelle, no meeting tonight. Switch to plan B: learn as much as you can, write him a quick "nice to meet you" e-mail, and go find a referral. She introduced herself to the five people remaining in the group. Hank Lyle scanned the group, muttered, "Talk to you later, ladies," and strode after Jordan.

Michelle watched him go. The woman next to her said quietly, "Well, *okay then,* Hank," and asked Michelle, "How do you know Sean?"

"I don't," said Michelle. "Do you?"

"We work together," she replied.

"Thanks for inviting me into the group," said Michelle. "I came here to introduce myself to Sean and ask about Chestnut's growth. Has it caused problems?"

"You can't imagine. It's great to grow, but what headaches!"

"Okay if I ask you about it?" asked Michelle.

"Sure," the woman said, holding out her hand. "I'm Diana Jasper, Chestnut's regional sales director for the Southeast." She looked at Michelle's name tag, and asked, "What do you do?"

"I'm Michelle Stevens, and I help sales teams become more effective. . . ."

If you're just entering a group, pick a lull in the conversation to introduce yourself. Don't interrupt. Sometimes, when people join a group with a high-profile person, they ignore the others and try to buttonhole their target. They only come off as rude or pushy, not the impression you want to give!

This is a moment of truth for many of you—will you join the group or shut down?

If you're feeling self-conscious or afraid of rejection, it's time to ask, what's the worst that can happen? That someone won't respect you? That someone will think you're desperate? That you won't find a great connection in the group? Frankly, most people are so preoccupied with themselves or so focused on their own goals that their rejection is nothing personal. (I'll say more about handling rejection in chapter 8.)

Eleanor Roosevelt said, "No one can make you feel inferior without your consent." Even if someone's behavior is insulting, they cannot humiliate you unless you accept their message. So tell yourself this is business, nothing personal, and get on with your networking. When you hit a wall, go to Plan B like Michelle in the example above—and to make it clear: Networking's Plan B is always to find new information and new connections. Don't let embarrassment shut you down!

Even if you do a really bad job, suggests Steve Harper of the Brenton Group, "Just apologize and say, 'I'm not very good at this, am I?' And you know what they'll do? They'll say, 'It's all right. What's your name?'"

If entering a group gives you cold sweats at first, introduce yourself to someone else who is standing alone. You're both there to talk and listen, right?

What Will You Talk About?

Fortunately, group settings give you a lot to talk about. Pick up on each invitation to start a conversation. Someone will say, "Hey, that was a great speaker," and you can say, "Yeah, what did you think about her predictions for the next five years?" Spawn the conversation, don't snub it.

Why not be open about the reason you're attending the event? "I'm really trying to broaden my contacts in this industry, and I came here because the speaker is an expert I want to meet."

I lead with my handshake: "Hi, I'm Jeff Taylor. I don't know anyone here but I'm trying to meet some new people." Sometimes just being that candid sparks an interesting discussion.

You can develop an entire style around introducing yourself, but just saying "Hi, I'm Bob Smith and I work at ABC Co." doesn't get much conversation going. Instead, lead with one of the questions you prepared in chapter 4.

Here's another way to come up with relevant information: mentally fill out the contact file you prepared in chapter 3 for each person:

- Who's their employer?
- What do they do?
- Who do they work with?
- What interests them most about their work?
- Who do you have in common?
- Why did they come to the event?

People love to talk about themselves and their work. This is the time when your genuine interest in meeting new people shines through. (If you're not really interested, that will shine through as well—so get interested!)

"What brought you here? What do you think of the host organization? How about that provocative point the speaker made at the end of her talk?" This professional small talk can lead directly into exploring the person's profession, connection to the event, and employer.

Many people sleepwalk through these events, but if you're awake to the opportunities you'll find connections in the most routine activities. For example, at the end of a presentation people often line up to meet the speaker, and if you're in that line, strike up a conversation with the people in front of and behind you. Ask what they think of the speaker's points, and take it from there. (When I speak at conferences, I have a bird's-eye view of this. Some people talk to others and end up laughing and having a great time, and by the time they get to me I have to interrupt them—they're enjoying the conversation so much they forgot they were in line to see me!)

Style Tip

You can adjust your tactics to suit your style as well. Here's an example: You're at a networking event and want to meet someone. Here are different introduction tactics, one for each networking style:

- Swan: Get help. Have someone introduce you, as Sarah introduced Martin to Ben. Here's another example, in which a friend introduces a swan-style networker named Cindy: "Cindy, I want you to meet Dan Gardner. You've been talking about writing an article about legal issues in your profession and Dan's an attorney who has been quoted in the news on the same issues." Dan doesn't have to know that Cindy did the research and then asked a friend to introduce them.
- Butterfly: I hardly have to tell you to go straight in! "Hi, I'm Sarah. I'm here to meet people and you three look like you're having a lively conversation. May I join you?"
- Dolphin: Comment on the event itself. "I'm amazed that I only know two or three people here. The organizers did a great job of mixing it up. My name's Luis. . . ."

- Lion: Focus on a topic. "I overheard you talking about call centers, and that's what I came here to discuss with people. My name's Michelle, and you're folks I have to meet."

Keep Moving

During the networking portion of a business event, you're expected to move around. Conversations shouldn't last more than ten or fifteen minutes. If things get really interesting, you can always schedule a deeper conversation by being up front: "I think we have a lot more to talk about, but I've taken enough of your time. Can we get some time to talk, maybe after this event or later this week?"

Susan RoAne, author of *How to Work a Room*, has another tip to move comfortably between groups. "When you leave a group, walk deliberately at least one-quarter of the room away. This signals you are not abandoning the group for a better one; you are simply making the most of your time."

How's your memory? Networking events can overwhelm you with people's names, faces, and stories, and the moment when you're between conversations is a good one for taking a few quick notes. This is where the small notebook helps to convert a single contact into an interesting relationship. Treat these conversations as short versions of the face-to-face networking you practiced in chapter 4. After a conversation, take just a moment to note what was said. Sometimes you can jot a note on the back of someone's business card, like this:

"Chip"   Spouse — Marcia (Marsha?);

daughter at Tulane

Big project — making Web site easier for
repeat business (B2B)

Follow up: Send Forbes customer Web tech
article

Translation:

- His card says Harold but everybody calls him Chip.
- His spouse's name is Marcia (or Marsha—didn't spell).
- He mentioned his daughter is a sophomore at Tulane.
- His current big project is a revamping of the company's Web site, making it easier for existing business-to-business clients to continue buying without a sales call.
- Follow-up: I promised to send him a recent article from *Forbes* magazine on the company that just completed a brilliant B-to-B customer interface.

This is more than enough information to follow up brilliantly. You'll show you do what you promise, and you'll put energy into making a new relationship.

In addition to notes, you can use this instant filing system, shared by expert networker J. Scott Hoyland: "When I go out to network, I use three pockets. My business cards always come from my right hip pocket. My breast pocket is where I put the cards of everybody that I'll follow up with: I've promised them information, a referral, or a call. Business cards of everyone else go into my left pants pocket—they're just going to my database, probably at a C-level priority, for now. Women can do the same with jacket pockets or three compartments of a purse."

Later, when you get home from the event, you'll dig out those cards and create a new contact file for each person. Then you **must** follow up, using the same methods you learned in chapter 4. Follow up right away, because the person you most want to add to your network may have met five other people at that event. Be the one they remember.

Whether networking is the purpose of the event or secondary, you have permission to make new relationships. Don't linger in the comfort zone of hanging out with your colleagues. Don't stay in the comfort zone of remaining a stranger. Introduce people you know to one another. Practice your personal brand statement when someone asks "What do you do?" Offer to help. You'll discover that the relationships you need to connect to your next job are in that room. And if they're not in that room, they'll be in the next room, or the next. . . .

Try This

Network with the self-employed! Go to a meeting focused on entrepreneurs, especially small-business owners. Groups like BNI or the Chamber of Commerce are full of self-employed people. They probably can't hire you, but they are some of the most accomplished networkers you'll ever meet. They talk the language of relationships and are usually very energetic in supporting others. And you can always offer to recommend them to your friends.

Want to find a focused networker? Talk to a person who has to meet a payroll!

Sometimes you'll think that you're wasting your time, or getting nowhere—but you rarely have enough information to make that judgment. So when you say, "I'm wasting my time here," automatically ask yourself, "Is it possible that out of all the people in this room, and all the people they know outside this room, there is nobody who can move me closer to the job I want?" Then keep hunting. Allow serendipity to play a part by just starting a conversation with someone. You made the effort to show up, and the worst that can happen is you don't go home with a hot lead.

The department store magnate John Wanamaker once said, "I know half my advertising dollars are wasted. I just don't know which half," and the same applies to your encounters in those rooms. Half your conversations may be wasted (although if you learn something, the conversation is worthwhile), but you don't know which half. So do yourself a favor and show up. After all, if you stay home, I guarantee you won't be networking!

EXERCISE 10

Get Your Kit Together

Before you go to your first large networking meeting, assemble the following simple networking kit, and keep it handy. It contains things that networking contacts commonly ask for (like a resume) and also information that helps the conversation move forward (like work stories). Finally, choose a couple of simple objects, like a good outfit and nice-looking notebook, which help you project a professional image.

- Clean copies of your resume.
- Business cards with phone and e-mail information (if you currently have a job, you may want to use a private e-mail address).
- A list of specific target companies—places where you think you might find a job.
- A list of potential job titles—to help contacts connect you to jobs.
- Several detailed, memorized stories about your work achievements (on index cards, as reminders).
- A professional business outfit for face-to-face meetings.
- A pen and notebook. Pocket-size is best for taking occasional notes or writing the address of someone who forgot their card!
- Comb, breath mints, and handkerchief.

Incidentally, you'll definitely need this kit for job interviews. You might as well get it together now, because you will soon be hearing about job possibilities!

Martin Makes Another Referral

To: Sarah
From: Martin
Re: Connection for you

Sarah:

Thanks for asking me to the networking event. Ben told me that he's talking to St. Clair Enterprise Software but he was interested to know more about my company, Axis Partners.

I found another name for you. Dawn Temple works as a vice president of product development at ELH, one of your target companies. I have met her only once but her husband Sam works with me, and if you like, I can e-mail him an introduction. Let me know.

Thanks for the invitation, but I don't think I will go to next month's networking event. I think you should spend a little more time online, because you can find people a lot faster that way. I would be willing to show you some of the Web sites for locating and connecting to people.

Regards,
Martin

6 Get Out of Your Box

The day you decide to start looking for a job, you should be able to e-mail 200 people with this message: "I just want to reach out to my friends, and tell you that I've left my company. I'm going to take two weeks off and then I'm going after new opportunities. I'll be calling each of you soon to ask about your company, your industry, and other employers you might know."

Do you have 200 people in your network yet?

You've talked to your comfort network. You've followed up with referrals. You've met some new people online—but the day comes when you need to find more contacts. Where else are you going to connect with people, so that you are prepared to send that e-mail?

Sarah Targets Dawn

"Yes, I know Dawn Temple," said Luis. "She's a partner at ELH. How do you know her?"

"My friend Martin introduced us via e-mail," Sarah answered. "I'm meeting her a week from tomorrow, and in the meantime, I'm asking everyone in my network if they know her."

"Good thinking. Dawn contracted us a couple of years ago to train her new business development team. . . ." Luis began. He went on to describe the business of ELH, Dawn's management style, and his experience at the company. Sarah took notes.

Luis finished with an offer and a question: "I'll be happy to call her on your behalf. No, wait—we've got time for a handwritten note." Luis took a note card from a pile on his desk and continued, "Dawn is well connected; does anyone else in your network know her?"

"Bridget McLarty and George Bass, who I met through Bridget, have told me they've met her," said Sarah.

"Good," said Luis. "Let me borrow that notebook." He took Sarah's notebook and wrote "Dawn Temple, ELH" in the center. "Let's make a diagram of the connections we know."

Sarah watched as Luis wrote "Michelle," "Martin," "Bridget," "George," and "Luis" around Dawn's name. "Anyone else?"

"There's a sales rep at ELH I met at an event. I didn't have much time to talk to her, but I could give her a call."

"That's a possibility," said Luis. He wrote "sales rep." He then wrote "Sarah" in a corner, and "Martin" nearby. He asked, "You met Bridget through Martin, right?" then drew.

When the drawing was complete, Luis traced the connections. "Solid lines represent relationships you established—with Michelle, Martin, and the sales rep. Double lines are referrals linking Dawn and the connections you know will recommend you. Here's one for me," he said as he connected the names Luis and Dawn.

Sarah considered, then said, "Martin would recommend me in an e-mail. . . ."

Luis shook his head. "Martin doesn't know Dawn. The recommendation is effective only if it comes from someone who knows you and knows Dawn."

"Okay, then I'll ask Bridget."

"Good. What about George?"

Sarah tapped her pen on his name. "I don't think George liked me," she said. "He didn't have any referrals."

"Can't hurt to ask," said Luis with a smile. "We'll put a question mark on the double lines for George and the sales rep.

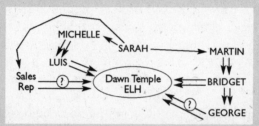

He went on, "I'd like you to come at her through several referrals before your interview. You've got me and Bridget at least, and you have four days to locate more."

"Isn't that just bugging her?"

"Not if your contacts can sincerely recommend you. Think about it: You could walk into the interview with four people already telling Dawn that you're the right person for the job. She has a by-the-book corporate style. She likes extra assurance, and I think she'll respond to the extra effort."

Whenever I meet someone new, I give their card to my executive assistant, Kaycee Langford; if there's no clear connection the card goes in a box on my desk. If the person's really interesting, the information goes right into my contacts file. Of the thousand cards I have in my box, probably 985 of them shouldn't make it to the contact database in my handheld computer—but 15 of them are part of my future. Five of them could change the course of my life. I just don't know which five . . . yet.

When it comes to networking for a job, your thinking might be trapped inside your own kind of box—the box of a safe routine. You live in a box called your home; you go to work in a wheeled box called the car (or the bus, or the subway). You step into a box called an office, cube, or desk at work. You meet with familiar people in a slightly larger box called a conference room. Then you get into your wheeled box and go back to your home box. And you wonder why your network isn't expanding?

If you've been keeping up with the networking plan in this book, by this point you've already recognized your comfortable little box. You have started working out from your comfort network (which meant pushing out beyond your comfort zone).

It's a good beginning and you've practiced some valuable techniques, but it's time to step out of your box and step onto unfamiliar networking ground and take the techniques you've learned to move your networking to the next level—making career connections not only through referrals, but through common ground. When you find common ground with someone, you have the basis for a networking relationship. This is the time when the networking habit begins to permeate through multiple aspects of your life—not just your work life, but your whole life.

You're about to take your networking into uncharted territory, and you'll start with the groups most strongly dedicated to career networking.

Professional Associations

Professional associations always have at least two purposes: the first depends on their particular mission, such as furthering the profession, and the second is networking. People join professional associations to learn, meet, exchange ideas, and work together toward common goals, such as the establishment of professional standards. They join not only to broaden their understanding of their industry, but also to broaden the number of people they know within their industry. Associations stage conferences, seminars, and other gatherings. This is a great place to network because conversation and exchanging information is the point! If you're skilled, thoughtful, and connected, you've got something to share. Many professionals use these associations to locate new clients as well as new job opportunities. For some, these associations have replaced their employer as the anchor of their professional life.

There's an association for every conceivable line of work, from accounting to zoology. If you can, find an organization that has chapters or holds events nearby—you want to get face-to-face. Google, MSN, and Yahoo! all maintain lists of associations. Weddle's, an information service for HR professionals, maintains a good list of associations on their Web site, **weddles.com.**

If don't know the name of professional associations in your area, try searching online using terms such as *organization* (as in "National Organization of . . ."); *society* ("American Society of Civil Engineers"); *federation* ("National Federation of Independent Businesses"); or *bureau, center, chamber, club, coalition, congress, council, forum, group, institute,* or the name of your state ("Missouri Society of Certified Public Accountants").

If you served in the military, get in touch with organizations affiliated with the service, such as the VFW, American Legion, or **military.com.**

Professional associations usually have membership directories (open only to other members) so once you have joined, you can mine a rich lode of contacts. Larger associations may also maintain databases of persons who are specifically networking for their careers, or who are interested in particular topics. Either way, the association becomes the "referral" in and of itself because you and your contacts are now connected by virtue of membership.

Professional associations often stage a variation on the career-networking meeting. For instance, a small group meets once a month at a hotel or other public venue to share leads and ideas strictly for the purpose of improving their performance on the job. Another variant: You're the finance director of a health care company, and you meet once a month with financial professionals from other industries to discuss common challenges in your work. The focus is not on getting a job, but you will simultaneously form relationships that can help you bridge your career from health care over to another industry if and when the time comes.

Professional associations also allow you to showcase yourself. One of the best ways to network is to become an expert at your job. Other people in your profession will want to ask you questions. They'll want to share what they know. They'll want to be part of your world. As you become known among your peers, more people will seek you out.

School-Based Groups

College alumni/ae organizations expand your potential network both vertically (people in your career who are more or less experienced than you) and horizontally (people in other careers). Graduates often feel a powerful connection between career and college, so the fund-raising and educational events staged by your college's local alumni/ae chapter are full of easily made connections. There's a great self-selection process going on here: People join their alumni/ae organization precisely because it's a way to stay connected, and you'll make new connections easily. These groups have a lot of presence on the Web and are always organizing events and programs through which you can meet other alums.

Fraternities, sororities, or other college societies like Phi Beta Kappa host national organizations and local chapters where you can pick up where you left off with old relationships, or create new connections based on common ground. And this time it's haze-free!

Service Organizations

Clubs like the Elks or Kiwanis are similar to college-based affinity groups. These groups have a range of missions as wide as all human society, but they have something in common: mutual support and service. If you're a member of such a group, you'll find other members ready and willing to help you connect to a new job, even though "networking" per se is not the mission of the organization. (You might have members already in your comfort network; I mention them here to point out that you might not have seen them as part of a wider career network.)

Local Business Groups

Local business groups are very direct about their ability to connect people on a professional level. These include the Chamber of Commerce in your town, and also groups with a specific industry focus—a local Ad Club, for example. You can also find groups that are based entirely on shared experience or mutual support, such as local organizations for veterans, or one of the many organizations focused on women in business. There even are a few national organizations that exist purely for the purpose of networking: Business Network International (**bni.com**) and Fast Company's Company of Friends (**fastcompany.com/cof**) are two excellent options.

Career center director Wendy Babson suggests a great way to take just one step out of your box: List people you know in work related to yours, but not directly competitive to yours. For example, if you're aiming for a job in real estate, you might list mortgage brokers, contractors, or architects you have known, all of whom do business with real estate companies. If you want a job as a building or facilities manager, look for people in maintenance, or vendors with businesses such as a coffee service, commercial cleaner, office supplies dealer, or office moving company. If you're aiming to be a call center manager, target people in telecommunications, IT/computer maintenance, office design, and sales.

Having said all this, you don't have time to get connected to every potential group, so when you're focused on career networking, there are a few criteria that will help you decide where to spend your (limited) time:

- Join groups that have a large membership, or that open the gate to large national organizations.
- Shop around. It's tempting to send in your $20 membership fee to join the first association you find, but do your homework—how successful are they as a networking milieu? (Hint: Ask current members.)
- Look for energy. Does the group have a large and active membership? Does it have staying power? Has it been around a long

time? Does it candidly state that one purpose for its existence is to bring members together? These characteristics distinguish thriving groups.

You also have to be sincere about your participation in any of these organizations. The person who joins solely to connect to a new job isn't in tune with the group's goals, so before joining six local groups, consider your motives and your ability to further the mission of the group. A certain church or temple in your town may count among its members very well connected professionals, but that alone is not reason to join!

Job Networking Groups

Organized job networking groups can be a huge benefit to anyone, from rank beginner to experienced networker. Often they're run by a career counselor, executive recruiter, or outplacement executive as a way of promoting a private practice. Sometimes they're run by state employment professionals; or they're started and maintained by entrepreneurial job seekers who saw a need for a group in their own search. Some have open memberships; some are highly exclusive.

The best groups are often small, ad hoc associations meeting in church basements or town hall rooms. They don't advertise, and as of this writing, there is no single national resource where you can locate a job search group in your local area. Some are active for a few years, then disappear or merge with other local groups. You can find local job networking groups through the "one-stop" centers run by state governments. Community event calendars and local bulletin boards will also list groups.

When they're good, job networking groups can work wonders, and when they're mediocre, they lead you nowhere. Each group will have its own personality. Leadership makes a big difference, so pay attention to how the group is run. Here are additional signs that a job search group, whether amateur or professional, is working effectively:

- It has an active membership, projecting a positive and professional attitude.
- Its leadership promotes a clear mission and procedures.
- It hosts a Web site or keeps a library listing local employment resources.
- It maintains good communication among members (Web mailing lists and e-mail newsletters are a good sign).
- Local employers and recruiters use the group to find job candidates.
- Its meetings include presentations about job search skills like employer research or interviewing skills.
- It brings in guest speakers with particular expertise in networking or other job search skills.
- Its members network actively, share leads, and continue to participate after they've landed in a job.
- It has operated continuously for a year or longer.

As you join a group (or two), consider also the diversity of its membership. You may feel more comfortable with a group of people working in your field, but a group dominated by one industry tends to have competition among members for jobs. Those groups also tend to produce fewer fresh contacts than groups representing a number of industries or professions.

I can hear you asking, "Why would I want to network with people who are out of work? They can't hire anyone." The answer is that people out of work still have a lot of contacts, they're motivated to network, and they have time to help. The sales director who lost her job last month can still introduce you to the finance director at her old company who's looking for an accounts receivable whiz like you (like any referral, you have to check out their relationship to the company—if that sales director was fired for incompetence, you might not want their introduction).

Members of job networking groups will give you the inside story of their former employers—where the perils and opportunities lie. Members might have even interviewed at your target companies already, and can give you tips on how their job application and interview process operates.

Within these groups, mailing lists make it possible to act quickly. A member can post a message: "There's an HVAC job listed at Austin Properties. Anybody have a contact there?" and shortly have a referral from another member in hand. Members are alert to job openings for other members. "I just talked to ABC Company and they didn't have anything for me but they're looking for someone like you." Imagine having fifty motivated people keeping an eye out for you!

High-level career-networking groups (for professionals and senior managers) tend to be more selective than volunteer-run groups. They might charge for membership (especially if they're part of a professional association), and have goals that go beyond finding work. They also might offer additional tools, such as:

- Large databases of managers and recruiters who will accept job applications from prequalified members.
- High-level connections among the membership.
- Formal, professional-quality training in work skills (e.g., public speaking) as well as job search skills.

Some groups specialize in a profession such as finance or consulting. There are local chapters of a few national networking groups, as well as groups run in association with outplacement or career-counseling firms.

Business networking groups that focus on generating customer leads can become a strong part of your career-networking plan; the networking techniques they practice support a lifelong career network. Selected professional networking groups can also work closely with employers and recruiters. Matt Bud, chairman of The Financial Executives Networking Group (FENG), explains, "A recruiter can send me a job possibility and they know I'll send it out only to qualified members under my name. People know who I am and the members of my group know the importance of my personal relationships, so they're respectful and only make serious inquiries."

Who Else Can Connect You?

If you have been working for a while, there are a couple of ways to connect to an "alumni/ae network" around your former employer. Networks of former employees started decades ago around a few large employers (such as IBM and TimeWarner). Now, these networks are Internet based, using Web sites, "groups" sections of Google, Yahoo!, and the like, and mailing lists to keep in touch. You'll have to do some digging; this is a relatively new phenomenon and takes place in a part of cyberspace that's still somewhat difficult to navigate. (In addition to the mailing list sites, you can search Web-based career networking sites under your company's name to locate past employees.)

"While you're considering reconnections with past work associates," suggests University of California career coach Matthew Temple, "work your way back through your resume, noting at each job the colleagues, vendors, and other contacts who you remember and respect. You can contact them directly, based on your previous relationship."

Is anybody you know from a former job fair game? Matt Bud suggests that "anybody from any company you've ever worked for is a good prospect. Even if they don't know you, they know of you. You have people in common. They will be much more open to helping you with this kind of connection than they would be to total strangers."

Even if you were laid off from a company, or quit a job under difficult circumstances, don't automatically write off your former colleagues. Once the emotions surrounding negative departures calm down, many people respond with genuine interest and a desire to help. Many of them will have moved on too, so track them down!

Look for "connectors" within the group. They are the well connected and the well known. They play strong roles in spreading ideas. Often they occupy a prestigious position in an industry, such as CEO of a major company—or maybe they lead your industry organization. Within groups, they are often the leaders, not only in name but in behavior, too. Longtime members identify them as persons who have been particularly helpful. They are the ones who promote the association's ideas, run the membership drives, or stay late to talk to newcomers.

Who are the connectors in your life, in your network? Remember that people you meet in Human Resources, operations, sales, and service industries like tax preparation or real estate often have a huge web of relationships. People who are successful in "contact jobs" love to share their expertise—and their connections. You'll also spot those folks who are natural centers of activity. There's an aura around them—authority, competence, self-confidence. They seem to make the conversation go. You'll notice this at tables during networking events or before the speaker comes on—one person who makes the event flow. You want to get to know that person; chances are they're a good networker.

Mentors can play a vital role connecting you to your next job. Like informational interviewing, mentoring is rewarding for both the person being helped and the helper. One job of the mentor is to connect a less experienced person with others, and that can continue long after the relationship has grown. If you've lost touch with a mentor from your past, get back in contact. One of the great things about keeping in touch with old mentors is that, as a more experienced person, you may be able to help them. Even if you can't pay them back, you can begin to "pay forward" the help you were once given by doing some mentoring yourself. The mentoring you do is exactly the kind of openhanded giving that fuels good networking.

Try This

Be the Star of Your Own Network

Ian Christie, founder of Bold Career (**www.boldcareer.com**), suggests that organizing and hosting your own networking events is a smart way to become a networking star quickly. Here's Ian's step-by-step guide to starting a career networking event:

1. Structure a formal, organized networking event at which each attendee gets less than five minutes to talk about him or herself and their problem or opportunity. Then the other participants contribute ideas, connections, advice, and referrals. At the end, attendees mingle.

2. Pick a spot where you can all sit at a table, or if it is a bigger group, fit into a room.

3. The success of your event will rest largely on the quality of the attendees, so make your guest list carefully. The best guests will be able to describe what they need clearly and concisely and will also have valuable suggestions or information for others. Decide whether you want your invitees to bring their own guests. If they do, you will be able to expand the group faster. Remember, however, you could lose control over who's coming.

4. E-mail a list of all confirmed attendees with a two- to four-sentence bio of each. Everyone should know a bit about who they will be meeting. Also confirm the date, time, and directions to the location. Send it to the group three to five days before the event and again the day before.

5. Be the prime connector. When the event begins, welcome everyone and introduce those who don't know each other. Begin and end the meeting on time. Control the clock so everyone gets a turn to talk. And don't forget to talk about yourself and what you're looking for.

6. After the meeting, follow up. Send an e-mail thanking everyone for attending and following up on any action items that came out of the meeting. Set a date for the next event. Make sure you personally follow up with the people you want to get to know better.

Once you've established yourself as the go-to person in your growing network, you will be able to feed off its contacts, energy, and ideas to build your career or business.

Targeting

Targeting an approach reverses the usual order of networking: you start with a person you'd like to meet and then create a link to them from your existing network.

In the course of your job research, you'll learn about people you'd like to meet from news articles, company Web sites, and other references for which there's no ready referral. You'll hear someone interviewed on drive-time radio and think, "I could work for that person."

You can make a connection with an executive by tracing a path back from them, like this:

1. I want to meet the CFO of company A.
2. On the "Clients" section of its Web site, company A lists company B. I will assume the CFOs know each other.
3. My friend Nancy works with the CFO of company B. I can ask if she will introduce me to the CFO of her company . . . and in addition to asking that person about company A, I can ask for other connections.

You can alert your network with a broadcast e-mail that you're seeking a connection to a particular individual. You can try to locate connections to that target person among all your various networking groups, professional or alumni/ae groups, and others mentioned above.

Diane Darling, CEO of Effective Networking, points out that when you target a person, you'd better have a good reason. "You need to know *why* you have to connect to them, and what is going to make them say yes, I'll talk to you. I make time for people who articulate very clearly the point of the meeting and put limits on their request. . . . if you're respectful of someone's time up front, you're more likely to get some of it."

Remember the steps you learned in chapters 3 and 4:

- Get your story together (your personal brand statement).
- Work through referrals whenever possible.
- Structure a conversation focused on rapport, a personal brand statement, and questions, offering help, and requesting further referrals.

Once again, your personal brand will help you here—if your network contains someone who can refer you, make sure they can pass along your fundamental selling points. What you want is an introduction like this: "Mary, I'd like to introduce you to Carol Jones. I know her through the beltway finance professionals' group. She's a talented and hard-working finance professional, and one of my star employees vouches for her. She's currently looking for a new position and told me that your company particularly interests her."

This referral is a little cool but businesslike, and the fact that a professional is confident enough to put their reputation on the line for you, does the job.

Multiple Referrals

If you find several connections to a target person, you might judiciously approach them from many directions simultaneously. Janice Dilworth, a professional recruiter at Washington Mutual, describes how she employed this technique to land a job several years ago:

> When I was targeting Washington Mutual I asked a banker about the company's reputation. I asked others how to approach the company. I asked everyone if they had a neighbor at Washington Mutual, or knew someone working there, or if they knew someone who had been a vice president there ten years ago. When I finally interviewed at Washington Mutual it turned out that a number of people had recommended me to the company over several months—not just employees, but vendors and alumni of the company as well. It was amazing.

Note the time frame: Janice was recommended by numerous people over the course of a few months. This is a key quality—your ability to inspire growing confidence in an employer's mind long before the job interview. It doesn't happen all at once and it's not the same as firing off fifty resumes to the HR department. Janet targeted a company, then went back to her network to discover connections to that company, and built a reputation for herself—and a relationship to the company—via trusted referrals.

Long-Distance Networking

Sometimes you might want to step out of your geographic box. Long-distance networking to find a job in another town, state, or country requires the same diligence as targeting an individual—you must dig deeper into your network to find the right connections.

If you're trying to move within the United States, ask to meet people who are connected in any way to employers in your desired location. Thus, if you want to move to Seattle, develop a list of target employers there and ask your network for referrals to people at those companies (in any location), to people in Seattle, to people at Microsoft, Starbucks, and Seattle-area recruitment offices, to people who used to work at Boeing headquarters before it moved to Chicago, and so forth. Remember that your connection to an employer may actually come through their branch office nearby (your fishing partner's son-in-law is a regional manager for Starbucks in your home town of Atlanta, and can refer you straight to the main office in Seattle).

You can do a lot of long-distance connecting via phone and e-mail (you can learn a lot in a twenty-minute informational phone interview). Face-to-face contact is still preferable, however, so get in front of people as much as possible, for example, by booking a week of networking meetings (four a day) in your new location. This makes for an intense week, but you establish a core network of twenty people, and their referrals can bring you to many, many more.

International networking became a lot easier with the adoption of Internet technologies. E-mail is ubiquitous; global research tools allow you to find key contacts. Company Web sites offer international job listings. You can search for job opportunities at international career Web sites (as of this writing, Monster is in more than twenty countries), and learn about working overseas at sites like **goinglobal.com**.

Peter Segal, a partner at Ogilvie and Associates in London, believes that U.S. business culture is currently more receptive to the direct approach: "In America people pick up the phone and talk to you. In parts of Europe, you'll still encounter two layers of bureaucracy deflecting you." Although business culture is changing in Europe and Asia, you'll also discover companies and countries where long-standing connections, such as those forged at elite universities, count a lot in the hiring process.

A long-distance job search has little room for chance meetings, so take the targeting approach. Says Peter Segal, "Work back from your endgame. Think, 'Who can get me to Fred Smith in London?' rather than just working your way through a contact list."

Whether you're networking 100 miles away or 3,000, broadcast details of what you seek to your current network; our society is so mobile that most of us have friends and colleagues a long way away. Re-examine your network for people who are working (or have worked) in the country you target:

- Alumni/ae and professional associations.
- Current or former employees of your company.
- People you have known at former employers.

(Incidentally, if your own overseas connections have lapsed, reconnect enthusiastically: expatriates are used to picking up acquaintances after a long time.)

When you relocate, you have a dual responsibility to establish a local network as quickly as possible and keep your old network alive with e-mail and calls. Stay close, even if you're far away.

Cold Connections

Although networking is meant to build on unbroken connections, there are times when the connection trail is pretty cold. For example, a contact will tell you that they knew the vice president of ABC Co. twelve years earlier but since then they've lost contact. They say, "I doubt she remembers me but you really ought to talk to her."

You can still use this as a referral by mentioning the relationship: "Allison Green, who worked with you at ABC some time ago, suggested we meet. I am an electrical engineer. . . ." It's not an intimate connection, but often you'll hear, "Oh, Allison! I lost track of her . . . how's she doing?"

Like Allison, you also have cold connections. A conversation will remind you of someone you haven't talked to in years, and you realize that they might be an excellent part of your network. Once you locate them, how do you make a long-lost acquaintance part of today's network? Warm up those cold connections with a request just as you would a referral, using additional reasons to get in touch:

- Tell them you'd like to ask for their advice.
- Note how you found them (via search engine like Google, or a newspaper or magazine article that reminded you of them).
- Get reacquainted with them—what are they doing now?
- Reconnect with others from the time of your acquaintance.

Get over embarrassment by being direct; apologize for falling out of touch, say you're making a commitment to stay connected, and ask for a conversation. You might also briefly tell an old acquaintance your history since you last spoke—that you moved to the Denver area, that you changed your profession from marketing to sales, and that you finally got that certification in project management.

This time, you're making a commitment to stay in touch. If you jump the chasm of years to reacquaint yourself, stay acquainted with an occasional e-mail, letter, or call. If you drop people the moment they stop being obviously useful, then you're just exploiting them.

The Cold Call

Occasionally, you'll target someone and you just won't be able to find a connection at all. Can you succeed with the telemarketer approach to stepping out of your box—just finding a name and picking up the phone for an ice-cold call?

Keith Ferrazzi, author of *Never Eat Alone*, says that true cold calling has no place in building a network, but that doesn't mean you can't bring a stranger into your network. "If you don't have a personal referral, you've just got to figure out a way to make it a warm call," says Keith. "In any case you mustn't reach out to somebody and only say, 'Hi, this is what I need from you.' That's all take and no give.

You have to first learn as much as you can about that person and their business, and go to them generously, saying, 'This is what I can do for you.'"

Your contribution doesn't have to be gigantic; its significance lies in the thought you've put into it. If you're a new graduate, you may think you have little to tell the senior VP of a food company, but consider how they'd respond to a proposition like this: "I've polled 100 students at my college about how easy (or hard) it is to find your product in stores, and put together a three-page summary of their comments. I thought you might like to hear their straight-from-the-street reactions to your store placement."

Sometimes, candidly, they don't need your help—but they may like doing a favor for someone who has demonstrated self-confidence, follow-through, and a professional attitude while making contact. People in positions of influence are bombarded by ill-considered requests for their time, but even people who don't do a lot of favors for strangers appreciate the respect you have shown by learning about them and their business.

Some business leaders simply like to help people find work, and they often suggest that the only thing you do in return is to help someone else when the time comes. If you're lucky enough to connect with a person like this, follow up the story of how you passed on their generous attitude (this kind of follow-up solidifies your original connection, and it's a darn nice message to receive).

Try This

Hold a Barn Raising

There's a one-time networking activity called a barn raising (after the barn raisings in farming communities; the films *Witness* and *Cold Mountain* have great barn-raising scenes). Here's what you do:

Gather ten to twenty people you know. They can be employed or looking. Give each an index card and pen. Pass your resume around, and allow everyone thirty minutes to read your resume and socialize with each other.

At the thirty-minute mark, stand up and deliver your personal brand statement to the group. Remember to describe exactly the work and connections you seek.

Then, ask people to write the following on index cards:

- Their name.
- The name, employer, and relationship of a person they're willing to introduce you to (Bob—ABC Co.—my college roommate).
- One additional thing they will do to help you—make one additional introduction; comment on your resume; send you a list of additional employers you haven't mentioned; send an article; recommend a book or Web site.

Then each person reads their index card aloud, and makes a public commitment to the help they'll give you. Their referrals don't have to be hiring managers—just someone who will be willing to network with you. For this one time, the group's focus is entirely on you. You can walk away from an evening like this completely re-energized, thinking way outside of your mental box.

(Here's a fun variation: Instead of using index cards, have people write on large sheets of paper and post them on a wall. Then everyone can read about everyone else's connections, which really gets the networking in gear.)

Make it a social event! Make it a potluck dinner, or coffee and dessert, or a cocktail party. A job barn raising not only opens new doors, but also reminds everyone present that we're all in this career thing together, and we can even have a good time getting to our goals.

Network Everywhere

For the career networker, getting out of the box is as much an attitude as an activity. The attitude is curious, adventurous, and open to new people coming into your life. Most important, that attitude is turned on 24/7. You can meet life-changing people in the most surprising places. You go to the symphony and strike up a conversation with the couple sitting next to you. You ask them out for coffee afterward. You find out not only that you enjoy the couple, but also that you have a common acquaintance who would be a nice lead for a job possibility. Maybe you've made a job connection; maybe you've made a friend. Maybe neither—but you've put yourself out there, and that's what counts.

Air travel is also a great opportunity: two strangers sitting inches apart for four hours. I'm rarely gregarious early in a plane ride because I need most of the time to work, but even if I'm busy, I try to use the last ten minutes to make some connection—so as the wheels go down, I'll say, "Hey, are you home or are you going to work?" They answer, and the small talk takes it from there. Maybe the conversation goes somewhere, and you find out you're sitting next to a stockbroker who lives two towns over and knows a great piano teacher for your eight-year-old daughter. Maybe you're sitting next to your future business partner. (Mealtimes on long flights are another good opportunity for an introduction.)

As I get up from my plane seat, I always give the other person my card and say, "Hey, if I can ever help you, here's my card." They give me one of theirs. Then as soon as I get in the terminal I write on the card: "Met this person on the plane July 27. Married, two kids, Sudbury . . . e-mail re piano teacher."

Sometimes you make a close connection with a person over a long period of time—say, standing on the sidelines of your kid's soccer games and chatting ten Saturdays in a row. One day you say, "I'm going for coffee; want one?" and you end up helping them hire their next sales manager, or finding a good baby-sitter, or connecting to a job 900 miles away.

Sometimes people need a push. For a long time, on that same field, I'd see the mothers of my daughter's soccer team sit together— no men. One day at halftime they were all up helping the kids, and when they came back to their chairs I was sitting in the middle. We all had a good laugh and I made some nice new connections that day. You have to shake up the routine sometimes to create that perfect networking scenario, because without a little push you'll never grow. So whether you're standing with the other moms (or dads) on the soccer field or standing with people from your own company at a networking event, your comfortable routine will only limit your possibilities—so make a habit of putting yourself out there.

Here's the habit in action: Find your own table at the event. Talk to the person you don't know. Walk to the other side of the room. When you meet a stranger, think, "This might be a person who changes my life—or I might be a person who changes theirs." Wouldn't it be fun to find out if that's possible?

EXERCISE 11

Check In and Review

If you've done even half of the networking I've described so far, you have a real career network in the making. Have you made 25, 50, or 100 contacts? How many face-to-face conversations have you had related to your job search?

Since networking is a long-term set of activities, it's good to check in from time to time. Review these questions and adjust—are you doing too much of one thing and not enough of another?

1. Do you have a contact file for everyone on your A-list?

2. Have you organized the information you got from notes, phone conversations, and other people's business cards—at least in some way you can understand?

3. Have you actually drawn a picture of at least one web of relationships, to see how the connections are made?

4. Are you following up with contacts you made in the early days?

5. Can you stand up and deliver a personal brand statement?

6. Have you offered help to people—and then delivered it?

7. Do you have a "networking kit" and routine ways to save information from face-to-face conversations?

8. Are you mixing up your activities and sources of contacts—some from friends, some from groups, and some from school or former jobs?

9. Can you articulate the strengths and weaknesses of your networking style?

10. Can you name two times you demonstrated your trustworthiness and sincerity through your networking behavior?

7 Internetworking

In the olden days, let's say fifteen years ago, a networking contact would tell you, "I'll introduce you to someone right away," and then they'd play phone tag for a week with that person. Or they'd say, "I'll write a letter on your behalf," and it would take two weeks before they found the time to produce that letter. Career networking was a slow-going process.

Today, that person can say, "I'll send an e-mail now to Joe, and you can call him this afternoon." Then they tap out a message while you ask questions about Joe. Wherever Joe is, he can get the message about you, and by that afternoon, you've made the appointment, which otherwise might have been lost among the hundred items on your contact's to-do list.

In the olden days, you heard about someone in a target company. You waited until Saturday to get to the library, where you slogged through reference books, old newspapers, and microfiche, looking for a mention. These days, you just type that name into a search engine, and up comes a wealth of information. Quick action is just one of the advantages the Internet has brought to networking; there are many others.

Today, career networking could be called "Internetworking." The Internet (which is one very big network) connects people to one another with such efficiency and ease that it could have been designed specifically for career networking. You can locate the people with whom you want to connect. You can find out all about them via Web pages and specialized networking Web services. You can contact them via e-mail, instant messaging, Web services, wireless, and other media. You can do all this in real time or at their convenience (this time shifting is critical for long-distance networking or reaching time-pressed people).

Sometimes your Web use is like fishing with a narrow-mesh net, catching a hundred names and sorting through them. Sometimes you throw in a single line and special bait to capture exactly the one fish you are after.

As Web technologies improve, you'll be better able to connect on a more and more personal level; but the fact is, the human part of the networking discussion—which is the really interesting part—is still up to you. To add Internetworking to your job search arsenal, your task is to learn and use Internet technology to handle information faster, organize it better, and use it more effectively.

For swan- and lion-style networkers, Internetworking is a godsend. It allows these somewhat introverted types full access to individuals before face-to-face encounters. If you identify with one of these styles, devote enough time early in your networking to master Internetworking sites and methods. For butterfly- and dolphin-style networkers, Internetworking is more an outlet for their extroverted tendencies— endless connections, endless possibilities.

The Dolphin Plunges In

Now that Michelle had connected to one of the senior people at Chestnut Systems, it was Luis's turn. He sat before his laptop in his favorite coffee shop, drinking a large black coffee and cruising the Net.

He entered "Sean Jordan" in the search field of the networking Web site, and then studied the result. Jordan was a sales guy, all right—even his online profile was a model of selling, and displayed numbers that would interest any potential employer. He's not shy about his success, and he expects to be checked out, thought Luis.

With a few more clicks, Luis found the kind of connection he was looking for: Jordan had previously worked at a company Luis knew well. Luis moved to his contact file and fired off a quick e-mail:

Hi Cathy:

First of all, I hope that intern I sent your way is working out—let me know if my recommendation was right for you or if you need more names. I seem to know a lot of graduates this year.

I've been trying to connect a colleague to Sean Jordan at Chestnut Systems, and I just found out that he worked with you at St. Clair software three years ago. Do you know him well enough to make an introduction? Drop me a line if you're comfortable with that, or if you need to know more.

Best,
Luis

Luis typed a follow-up reminder into his calendar, and then went back to studying Jordan's online profile. He and Michelle were definitely going to get in front of the guy.

You, Online

Just like networking in the physical world, Internetworking begins with putting yourself out in front of other people. In cyberspace, that consists of both "pushing" yourself directly toward others and making it possible for others to "pull" information about you in the form of a resume, a personal Web page, or a blog.

E-mail is the most common Internetworking tool. You send e-mail to people at every stage of the game, whether you're introducing yourself or keeping in regular touch with your network. E-mail is great for shy people. It feels much safer to contact someone that way. E-mail, however, doesn't have the impact of face-to-face conversation. If it's driving you toward a conversation, overcoming barriers of time and distance, then e-mail is taking its rightful place in your networking plans. If you're using it to avoid real dialogue, or if it's preventing you from becoming really involved, you'll find that it is less effective.

E-mail enables you to reach out and respond quickly, and that's an advantage when you've just met someone. You can continue the relationship while you're fresh in their mind. (It's also an advantage in a world where hiring can take place very quickly.)

Out on the leading edge of the Internet communications revolution, wireless handheld computer connections (and cell phones) allow you to network whenever you want. There are downsides to being connected 24/7, but for busy people this technology is a great advantage. It removes time restrictions. I used to spend the first hour of my day doing just a bit of my e-mail—not good. People with a quick question had to resort to putting sticky notes on my door to get my attention. Now that I carry a handheld with a private e-mail address, I can give answers instantly (and still find time to help people by forwarding their resume to an appropriate person).

Posting your resume online should be an early part of your job search and is integral to career networking. But it's an indirect approach to making connections, because you have to be found, rather than directly seeking a connection with someone. If you post your resume on a personal Web site, it will get picked up by the search engines, and it will come up as a match when employers use those engines to cull for documents containing specific terms like "Marketing" and "Copywriter" and "Chicago." Be aware that if your resume is open to all parts of the Web, anyone can get access to the information (that includes potential employers and anyone else, from long-lost friends to e-mail spammers).

Career Web sites like Monster and others are more targeted venues for career networking because employers have to pay to get access to the resume database. You can control how much information is revealed as well, so your privacy is better protected.

Career Web sites are also beneficial because they make it possible for potential connections to find you through your skills. For a recruiter searching for people, it's like being at a party where everyone's wearing a billboard listing their skills and experience. The recruiter can go to the person who interests them most and start talking. And the employer can search on any term. Some search the "experience" sections of resumes for company names on the theory that an ABC-type person will work out well at XYZ Co. I knew a financial manager who discovered that marathon runners had characteristic disciplines that translated extremely well for his workplace, so in addition to searching for resumes with financial skills he searched for the term "running marathons." He was jump-starting the process that usually occurs through many networking conversations.

Is this networking? Yes, if it gets the conversation going. Remember that one way to add connections to your network is to be open to the people who contact you.

Applying for a job online is straightforward outreach to an employer, but it can go beyond that. Career center director Wendy Babson points out that the information you glean from the posting can be another trigger point for networking: "You see that job listing, and brainstorm with your contact list, asking, 'Is it possible that I know somebody or someone that works for that company that can hand-deliver this resume as well?'"

Personal Web sites can serve you well throughout a career networking program. They are your version of a company Web site. Most Internet Service Providers offer personal Web hosting, with simple software for building a personal site. On your site, you should include your resume (with address and phone number removed for privacy), as well as the kind of statement you developed in chapter 3—an introduction to who you are, what you do, and what kinds of connections you seek. You don't have to state that you're looking for a job—remember, this is a tool to cultivate relationships—but include information about people you would like to meet or positions you'd like to know more about.

A personal Web site is useful when people in your network want to "pull" information about you, for example:

- It serves as a *24-hour reference* when a contact or employer wants to check you out (they may remember your name but have lost your card).
- It's a place to send contacts when you follow up after a conversation. Close your e-mail with "If you'd like to know more, visit my Web site at **www.yourname.net.**"
- You can say more than you can on a resume. For example, many people list useful Web resources in their professional field, or feature interests outside of work. It's an opportunity to become more interesting to a potential contact.
- It makes referrals more interesting: "Hey, Mary, I think you should meet Penelope de Angelo. She grew up in Chicago, just like you, and she's also in your field of work. Check her Web page at this address and tell me if I should introduce you."
- You're gonna get Googled. Wherever I go, employers and networkers tell me that they check out a new name on a major search engine like Google, MSN, or Yahoo! Why not have something that *you've* created pop up?

Web logs or "blogs" are a currently popular form of personal Web sites. Essentially, a blog is a personal online journal that you update regularly. People find out more about you by reading what you publish. If you can write well—and if you actually have something to say that potential contacts will find interesting—you might want to create your own blog. Currently, the blog culture is wild and woolly, and there's some risk of turning people off as well as turning them on. You can find out more about how to create a blog at **www.blogger.com, www.typepad.com,** or the major search engines at Google, MSN, and Yahoo!

For career networking, your blog has to be interesting and relevant to your work. You have to project a professional image. Your interest in rare books may be relevant to your work, and even your love of running may display traits that a potential employer wants to find. Your political views or the tale of your serious illness are not going to interest a potential employer; in fact, they may drive that employer away. Remember that what you put in a blog is all public property, and if your personal Web site or blog is not about your professional concerns, keep it separate from your career networking. (You can find an example of a work-oriented blog at **http://monster.typepad.com/ monsterblog/.**)

Message Boards and Online Communities

The next level of Internetworking brings you into the galaxy of online communities. Their roots run right back to the online "chat rooms" of the 1980s and 1990s, on services like AOL and CompuServe, and the services evolved from all-purpose, simple message boards to single-topic communities. Their growth was driven by the need for people (mostly technical people) to share information. Once in a while the conversation would be disrupted by a "flame war" of insults, but hey, that was the Web in those days. The thing to note was that people were connecting.

Posting messages is almost too easy. To sort out the best ways to use these services, it helps to tie them back to offline activities:

- Connect to the right people—and get face-to-face (or on the phone) with them.
- Keep the focus on building a career network.
- Keep offering something of value.
- Get referrals to the right people in their career networks.

With that in mind, let's work our way up the technological ladder from the simplest to the most complex online communities.

In the early days of message boards, someone in company A would notice that someone in company B posted really intelligent answers to questions and after a time they were e-mailing each other, talking about their companies. Recruiters started to cruise the boards looking for talent, and learned that if they participated regularly in message boards concerning their specialty (such as technical writing, finance, or operations management) they could find highly qualified people who were not looking for work. These were ideal long-term candidates, and so the recruiters would e-mail that person and strike up a relationship.

These message boards still exist all over the Web, but there are so many of them, used by so many people, that you could spend all day posting messages and not connect with the right person. The world of online discussion groups has grown so large, and is so prone to disruptive users, that the best policy is to find groups that have highly focused memberships. Open discussions such as Google Groups, AOL, MSN, or Yahoo! are stuffed with postings irrelevant to career networking.

There is still a role, however, for these large services: They make it possible for you to start your own online special-interest group right in the "Groups" areas. As of this writing, the service is free—just go to the group or community area and follow the instructions to create a new group.

Dave Asprey, an independent consultant, describes the experience of starting a group of alumni/ae from an old employer of his: "I told thirty former colleagues that I had started a group where people who were former or current employees could communicate with each other. In four or five months I had a hundred people participating. During that time I had to send frequent messages, point out job leads, and so forth. It's manageable traffic—one or two messages posted a day—but it puts me at the center of a group of people who are actively networking."

Dave goes on to describe how this small, private board can still make career connections: "Recently I needed to get in touch with senior executives from the type of company that members of my group did business with. I posted a message that said, 'Hey, I'm looking to meet people who do business with you in the following areas. . . .' Within a day I had fifteen people who said, 'I know people in this company at this level, what do you want me to do?' Three days after that I had set up meetings with the executives."

The first step of effective Internetworking via online communities is to sort through the maze of possibilities by identifying Web sites where you already have common ground:

- Online communities of professional associations (such as those discussed in chapter 6). Their Web sites host message boards, often available only to members.
- Online communities of schools or companies of which you are an alumnus. (Universities and graduate schools are becoming especially good at this.)
- Online discussion boards in your profession you could contribute to. These are hosted by career Web sites, and by companies trying to build communities of users around their products.
- Special-interest Web sites that appeal to you. There seems to be a site for every possible interest, so focus on the ones where you can form relationships based on real connections. An example: Military.com (**www.military.com**) for service personnel, veterans, and their families.
- The sites of service clubs such as Rotary International.

Just like face-to-face networking, Internetworking requires listening, learning, and offering help where you can. Answer questions posted on the message board. Share information. Keep your tone professional and don't make personal remarks in public. If you want to talk to one individual, e-mail them privately (many message boards supply an e-mail address with each message).

Career Networking Web Sites

The last few years have seen the rise of Web sites devoted purely to career networking. These online services have distinct advantages:

- They are focused: people join them to advance their careers (as opposed to dating, selling, or pursuing hobbies).
- The Web sites are designed to facilitate dialogue relevant to career networking, so online relationships can form quickly.

- They are designed to automate many of the information management tasks that can make networking so time-consuming, thus leaving you with more time for the conversation.
- They offer various levels of privacy—you can keep your address and even your full name confidential.

In addition, some of the services provide an offline referral system; you meet people through mutual acquaintances, and you can be reached only through someone you know. This mirrors effective face-to-face networking.

Career networking sites give you confidence because they are full of people interested in meeting, sharing information, and becoming useful. Like professional events, everyone's there to network, so you don't have to feel like you're intruding. Even within the focus on careers, you have lots of choices. There are sites that specialize in one type of work, sites that specialize in contact management, and sites that use chance encounters to a greater or lesser extent. But just as in offline networking scenarios, you have to participate actively and often if you're going to reap the rewards.

Scores of networking Web sites have sprung up in the past couple of years. Some are dedicated to finding work, some are really about generating leads for salespeople, and some are about personal matters like dating or finding old school friends. The career networking sites tend to blend purposes—they are not just intended to help you find a job, but also to help you do your work once you have a job. Different sites put more or less emphasis on business activities like locating potential clients, finding answers to business questions, locating potential business partners, and the like. There is rarely a hard line between finding work and doing work.

Here's a list of popular and well-designed services; visit and experiment with them to find which work for you. (These sites change often, so keep alert to new features and services over time.) They can be particularly useful for career networking:

- LinkedIn (**www.linkedin.com**)—emphasis on making contacts.
- Monster Networking (**my.monster.com**)—emphasis on career networking.

- Spoke Software (**www.spoke.com**)—currently focused on sales professions.
- Visible path (**www.visiblepath.com**)—currently focused on sales professionals.
- Ryze (**www.ryze.com**)—social and career networking featured equally.
- Meetup (**www.meetup.com**)—coordinates face-to-face meetings on all topics.
- Professional community sites of all kinds such as MediaBistro (**www.mediabistro.com**) or The Project Management Institute (**www.pmi.org**).
- **www.thesquare.com**—networking for graduates of forty prestigious universities.
- EntreMate (**www.entremate.com**) for entrepreneurs.

A couple of cautionary notes as these new networking services evolve: It's easy for someone to claim that they have a million connections online, but are they helpful, relevant, and trustworthy? Offline, you build a web of relationships through a series of face-to-face meetings. You come to know each individual before giving and receiving referrals. Online, you are tempted to assume the best and unfortunately, there are people out there who take advantage of online situations to solicit private information. Never give a home address, Social Security Number, credit card information, driver's license ID, or other personal information to someone unless you can confirm they are who they say. If you decide to meet an online acquaintance in person, use a safe public place. (This is simply sensible and professional behavior.)

Although online networking collapses distance, making it easy to share contacts with someone 800 miles away, it also slows down the conversation if you rely on e-mail to communicate. As you form more interesting relationships with individuals, it's helpful to get on the phone and communicate in real-time conversation. Even if you can't read someone's body language over the phone, conversation is more revealing, insightful, and spontaneous than e-mail.

There's a democratic spirit to online career networking. Your age, weight, and appearance are not instantly visible to trigger people's prejudices (and vice versa). You are judged on whether you are helpful, trustworthy, and well connected. Online introductions are less formal, but to be effective, focus the content of your discussions on the steps you learned in chapters 3 and 4: build rapport, communicate a personal brand statement (this may be built into the online services "profile" feature), ask questions, offer help, and request further referrals.

There are also "social networking" communities that focus on non-work relationships. Examples include Classmates, eHarmony, Friendster, Match.com, Military.com, MySpace, and Tickle. These sites are growing quickly and, although they are evolving beyond their early focus, at the time of this writing they are more suited for the "social" side of networking than serious career work. But you may examine them with your eyes open. If your networking has a social aspect in addition to career goals, don't discount these social networking sites, because an encounter there can be like that chance encounter on the airplane or the bus. If you strike up a conversation, things will happen.

Internetworking powers the detective work of networking. You'd like to reconnect with an interesting person you worked with three jobs ago? Search for them online—with Google, the career networking sites, or other search engines. Research the "About Us" sections of target companies' Web sites, where you'll find the biographies of company officers. When you identify common ground, such as the fact that you went to the same school as the HR director of a target company, you can put your connection engine into gear.

Try This

Give three networking Web sites a try in the next week—budget one hour of exploration time for each. Create a personal profile, and play around with some cool features like e-mail introductions. When you find one or two that work for you, schedule a regular thirty-minute visit on Monday, Wednesday, and Friday mornings for the next two months. You will experience a universe of new potential connections, which at the very least reminds you that there are literally millions of people out there making connections that help them advance their lives! Join them.

Stay on Track

Finally, there's a tempting but insidious downside to online networking—you can trundle along, posting and reading, posting and reading, and sometimes it is easy to lose focus on your purpose. You can spend hours playing online instead of really networking. Lurking at a site is not the same as forming relationships. Asking for favors is not the same as offering them. Sitting by your computer is just one activity of career networking, so while you should use Internetworking to expand your connections, do not let it become a substitute for face-to-face contact.

The Swan Connects Online

Martin completed his online profile in thirty minutes. He had included every possible connection he could remember, down to the name of his high school. Now it was time to play.

Easing back into the chair, laptop balanced on his thighs, Martin typed "Rensselaer Polytechnic Institute" into the search field of the online networking site. A moment later, 146 names appeared on the screen. Martin scanned them, recognizing several classmates. Ben's name was there, and no surprise—Ben had suggested Martin join this online site.

That's interesting, thought Martin. Ben told me that he was working at Chaffee Online Development, but it's not listed here. His profile's out of date.

Martin clicked on the e-mail address below Ben's name, and wrote in the e-mail window: "Ben, this is Martin Walters. I just joined the service you mentioned and saw your profile, but it doesn't mention Chaffee . . . ?? Did I get the name wrong?" He sent the e-mail and turned to the profiles of Rensselaer classmates. Several worked at companies he knew nearby. Martin wrote quick e-mails to them as well.

As he finished his third e-mail, Martin saw a reply from Ben arrive in his e-mail box. The message read: "Hey there. Sorry for the confusion. I'm doing a freelance project for Chaffee now, but looking for an executive job in the meantime. Can I talk to you about that?"

Martin considered for a moment, hit the "reply" button and wrote "Call me now," and then sent the reply. Before he could go back to searching on the site, Martin's cell phone rang.

"Hi, this is Ben Singer. Is this Martin?"

"Oh, hello Ben," said Martin.

"Right away I have to tell you," said Ben, "I don't know about any jobs at Chaffee."

"I'm not looking for a job," said Martin. "I'm looking for a new boss, preferably not a jerk. Want to talk?"

8 Roadblocks, Potholes, and Detours

Networking is a human web of relationships and conversation, and despite your best efforts to control it, a career-networking plan always runs into some surprises. For example, you'll be devoted to one target company for two weeks, and then discover that its competition has much better opportunities. Then there are pleasant surprises: you'll be intimidated by the thought of meeting with a company president, only to discover that person is a warm, interesting person . . . who's interested in you.

Toxic Hank

Sean Jordan rose as Diana Jasper led Michelle and Luis into his office.

"I am so glad to meet you," he said, taking Michelle's hand. "And I'm sorry to behave rudely the other night. Hank Lyle has been, shall we say, a little too persistent."

"You mean he's a pain in the neck," said Diana. She explained to Michelle and Luis, "He's a direct competitor of yours, and very aggressive. He targeted us for sales force training two months ago and won't take no for an answer."

"Lots of calls and e-mails?" inquired Luis.

"E-mails, calls, requests for us to join his online address book, calls from strangers endorsing his work, you name it," said Diana.

"Toxic networking," said Michelle.

Diana laughed, and said, "Exactly. I'm glad we had a chance to talk afterward without him."

"Toxic is the word," said Sean. "Lyle and a lot of other people are in our faces right now, trying to sell us services we don't need." He spoke to Luis. "Getting a note from Cathy is different," he said. "I'll see anyone she introduces."

"She told me you worked closely together at St. Clair Software, and I think she's very, very talented," said Luis.

"She's successful, too," said Jordan. He motioned for Michelle and Luis to sit, and continued: "Diana told Michelle a little about our sales force expansion, and you might be the right people to help." He strode to a whiteboard and began to diagram his sales force plans. "Here's the challenge we face. . . ."

The networking road to your destination has its share of roadblocks, potholes, and detours. If you imagine that every moment of your career networking will be fabulously rewarding, you'll be disappointed. You have to prepare for typical problems like rejection, bad matches, or boring events, and even annoyances like the toxic networker Hank who interfered with Michelle's networking (and lost an opportunity in the process). When you actively work your way through trouble, as Michelle did, your networking program will continue to thrive.

Toxic Networking

Put yourself in the place of a hiring manager in this situation, described by Monster senior contributing writer John Rossheim: "You get a call or an e-mail from a friend of a colleague, asking for a meeting with a murky agenda. Not wanting to offend your colleague, you halfheartedly agree to a brief encounter. The day arrives, and so does the feckless schmoozer. Though he still seems unsure of what he wants, he spends forty-five minutes jabbering about himself and assuring you that you're ideally suited to manage his job search and maybe even offer him a job yourself."

Don't be that feckless schmoozer! Rossheim lists the major causes of toxic networking:

- Toxic networkers are all take, take, take and no give.
- Toxic networkers project a downbeat, desperate demeanor: "*Please please please* network with me!"
- Toxic networkers set meetings with false pretenses: asking someone to lunch "to discuss an opportunity" and then hitting them hard for a job.
- Toxic networkers never follow up, even with a thank you.
- Toxic networkers consistently cross the line between persistence and pestering.

Although networking opportunities exist everywhere, you must be especially careful in casual settings. Even if the president of your dream company is standing next to you on the soccer field, you're welcome to have a conversation—but don't bring the subject around to work in the first ten minutes. Get to know the person; demonstrate that you aren't just there to bug them for a favor. And give them a break, too: you're not showing confidence by chasing them around the field.

Another version of overdoing it starts with your comfort network. A friend may not want to introduce you to their employer for any number of reasons—perhaps they're not impressed with your skills, but just as likely, something's happening at work that they cannot discuss, or their last referral blew up. Don't strain your friendship; drop the subject and when the right time comes, they'll remember.

Because networking puts you in close touch with otherwise un-connected people, you can fall into a tricky personal situation. For example, you may inadvertently learn confidential information or be privy to more than one version of a story. Sometimes a contact will pressure you to reveal private information. The rule of thumb is to remain discreet at all times. Don't talk out of turn, and don't burn bridges. Remember, you are nurturing relationships in your network, and your reputation is the only currency you have to spend.

Overfamiliarity is another inadvertent slip networkers make all the time. Even if you have an introduction, addressing a stranger as "Dear Jane" in your first e-mail can appear unprofessional. The simplest tactic is to write "Dear Ms. von Mehren," and wait for your referral to say "call me Jane." If you're not sure whether to sound formal or familiar, you can write "Dear Jane (if I may)." Little considerations like this build a positive impression, which gets you closer to that conversation.

That goes for conversation, too. What's more annoying than a stranger who uses your first name in every paragraph—"Jeff, I think we should meet for coffee because, Jeff, we have a lot of things in common, including our mutual friend Bill. Right, Jeff?"

Sometimes good networking techniques can be overdone. For example, does your personal brand statement sound a little too rehearsed: "Himyname'sJeffIcreatevaluablemessagestohelppeoplemaketheir livesbetterI'mlookingforapositioninmarketing. Who do you know?" Networking is an opportunity to sound natural, not to air your commercial—so slip your personal brand attributes into the conversation naturally.

It's fine to say you're in transition; it's not fine to appear ashamed of it. Steve Harper of the Brenton Group mentions this common bump in the conversational road: "It's frustrating to meet someone at an event who has a name tag with a company name like Myconsulting.com. I ask, 'What's Myconsulting.com?' and they say, 'Well, I kinda got laid off so I'm in transition so I'm really just looking for a job.'

"It's an immediate turnoff," says Steve. "If you're looking for a job, tell me you're looking for a job. Put it on your name tag. Then we're having a conversation."

If you are the object of a toxic networker's attention, set limits on the contact. Tell them that you can talk on the phone for fifteen minutes but not meet for lunch. When you're buttonholed at an event, say, "Excuse me, I'm trying to meet as many people as possible tonight so I'm going to mingle a little." Explain that you are careful of your reputation and make referrals only for persons who seem like good matches ("I'd love to help you, Mary, but I've heard your story and I don't feel comfortable introducing you to the CEO of my former company"). Do not allow someone to abuse your network connections or your willingness to help.

Rejection

Some people are just going to say no. They don't want to talk with you or network with you, or give you two minutes of their time.

Nobody manages rejection very well. Early in my career, I had to make a lot of sales over the phone. Nineteen times out of twenty, the answer was no. I succeeded with some simple attitudes:

- Decide that every rejection gets you past one of those nineteen "no" answers, and thus moves you closer to that twentieth answer—a "yes."
- Learn from every rejection. Could you have approached the referral differently? Did you have something to offer them? Harness the moment of rejection to spot weaknesses in your networking habits.
- Don't take it personally. Instead, talk back to rejection: "Okay, at this time they do not need what I have to offer, and the best thing to do is leave a good impression."
- Immediately after a rejection, get back in circulation. Turn to another group at the networking event. If you're home, get on the phone! Send another e-mail!

As you get busier, you'll say you have a lot of irons in the fire. My image of that expression is a cowboy's fire with branding irons—you have to put yourself and your networking habits into the fire of the marketplace, and let things heat up. The more irons you have in the fire at one time, the better chance you have of connecting to a job!

Sometimes you'll be rejected by a gatekeeper (usually your target's assistant). Protecting the boss's time is part of their job, so don't take it personally, and don't assume the initial "no" can't change eventually. An encounter with a gatekeeper is a terrific opportunity to change the usual networking game. See the gatekeeper as a resource in themselves. Gatekeepers are often the best-connected people in a company; it's their job to know everyone, yet most outsiders blow right past them. Since they are well connected and can be influential, why not ask them a few questions?

You must behave with respect and sincerity toward all gatekeepers; they are targeted by bad solicitors all the time, who feign interest then drop them. They are familiar with this second-class treatment, so the consideration you give them is memorable.

Silence from your target or the gatekeeper is another form of rejection. You send an e-mail, leave a voice message, and follow up, but you don't hear back. How hard should you try? Diane Darling, CEO of Effective Networking, suggests you apply the old "three strikes and you're out" rule. After three approaches, leave a final message mentioning the referral, like this: "Susan James, who thought we should have a conversation, mentioned that you are very busy. I'll let Susan know I've asked for an appointment, but we haven't connected yet and I'll follow up at a later time." This approach is both cordial and persistent—you've said you won't pester them but they're not quite off the hook. If the silence persists, put another iron in the fire and turn your attention elsewhere.

Diane also points out a particular form of silence—the dropped connection. Perhaps you worked with someone in the past, and kept in touch, and you even met with them as part of your new job search. And then they just fall off the face of the earth. You call, you e-mail—no reply. You could drive yourself crazy trying to figure out what's wrong, but the best policy, again, is to let it go and move on. Sometimes the relationship will come back much later, as it did for Diane:

"This person I liked a lot just stopped replying. I thought, something's amiss, or something's happened personally—but at the end of the day, I had to let it go. Two years later I appeared on the news, and that day I got an e-mail saying, 'Diane, I feel awful. I just saw you on the news and remembered I haven't returned your call.' He felt so guilty I could ask for just about anything I wanted!"

Try This

Now I'm going to ask you to do something that might seem to contradict everything I've said so far: make your contact list smaller.

I want you to prioritize your contact list to more accurately reflect your current web of relationships. Go through your list and be relentlessly honest about the quality of each networking relationship. If you see a person who won't return your calls listed as an A-level contact, change their priority to B (or even C).

Also, be honest about old addresses. Some people have a sentimental attachment to old contact information—they keep records of people they haven't seen in twenty years! If you want to do this, fine—but put them in a separate category from a networking contact list. One good category for these: "Update." That category means you want to track down the person, or take them completely off your list.

You might want to create categories in your contact list that are totally personal to you. I have a special list in my PDA called "guys who matter," and they're mostly just people I'd like to see socially. When I feel like going out with friends I haven't seen in a while, I just open up that category and give them a call.

Bad Match

You are going to get bad referrals from time to time. With the best of intentions, friends will introduce you to someone who doesn't want to see you, has nothing to offer you, and can't be bothered to help. Sometimes the person's actually hiring—but they're not hiring you. Sometimes your new contact can't even remember the person referring you!

Bad matches also happen with employee referral programs: Either the employee is excited when the person makes the referral and is then disappointed when the person doesn't get the job, or the employee is not really that psyched about the person they're referring. In the second case, the employee's in a double-bind. Either the referral gets hired, and ends up working with the referring person, or the referral doesn't get hired and this reflects poorly on the employee.

These bad matches test your forthrightness. When the professional person recognizes a bad match, he or she thinks, "Okay, perhaps this will be a short conversation," and asks a couple of questions. Sometimes just naming the bad match aloud helps the conversation branch off in a fruitful way. ("Hey, maybe this wasn't a perfect idea, but as long as we have ten minutes, let me ask about what you do. . . .") Remember that, at the very least, the person you're talking to has a network of his or her own, and may be willing to refer you to someone more appropriate.

These are the complexities of networking. The reality of human interaction is that we all have different personalities and different skill sets, and not every meeting will be as productive as the best. What separates a strong networker from a weak one is the determination to find mutual gain in any encounter (even an unpromising one), and a willingness to change course.

The Morgue

Some networking events can feel like nightmares. Full of anticipation, you arrive at the meeting of the Beltway Networkers Group and then . . . dead silence. You don't meet anyone, or worse, you keep meeting people with no discernable information, referrals, or needs. Maybe the speaker is incredibly boring, or only 5 people show up, or 300 people are crowded in a room with capacity for 200. Sometimes you growl, "I paid fifteen bucks and drove ninety minutes to come to this? What a waste of time!"

Networking then is like digging in a mine. You have to shovel 3 tons of earth to yield 1 ounce of gold. The gold is worth the work, however, so this is the time for determination and a last-minute save. Often these "disasters" are actually opportunities you don't yet perceive, like the times when you're two-thirds of the way through an event and haven't introduced yourself to one new person. Focus on that goal of having a good conversation with just one new person. Move away from conversations with people you know. Find a stranger.

Look for a way to be helpful, even if you're just setting up chairs or opening the pizza boxes. Always return to the magic question, "Who can I help, and how?" The only way to know that is to reach out again, and again.

If you're shy, **every** networking event feels like a potential nightmare. Your fear of failure can be self-fulfilling, but it's misdirected. Susan RoAne, author of *How to Create Your Own Luck*, observes that "shy people are some of the best people at events. Number one, they're not scanning the room while they're talking to you. Second, shy people don't show up and make a grand entrance or hog the limelight. Third, shy people are just as capable of good networking etiquette and follow-up as anyone, if they've prepared. Networking isn't the same thing as working a room. You can be a great networker and still want to throw up every time you enter an event."

There's a more insidious form of networking nightmare—discouragement. In *Monster Careers*, I noted that job searches are just plain hard work, and you have to find ways to refresh, recalibrate, and rethink your plan. Networking offers a way out, because you can always find a new person to talk to, get new information, and ask for help finding new paths toward your goal. When people respond positively, when they're helpful, hope and encouragement follow.

Is This NETWORKING or Just a Bad Date?

Except for the kiss, the similarities between a bad networking conversation and a bad date are startling:

"He got here late. Doesn't he care?"

"That person had bad manners/clothes/breath."

"She had nothing to say."

"He talked too much."

"She was a poor listener."

"I just didn't feel any chemistry."

"I couldn't wait to say 'goodbye'."

"Sure, I'll keep him in mind . . . not."

Get the etiquette down . . . and give them a reason to start a relationship!

These Are Not Networkers

You'll meet all types at a networking event, and you'll wonder why some of them bothered to come. Here are a few non-networkers I've noticed. Don't be one of them!

"Fat Albert"—He goes to a networking event only to eat (hey, go to dinner instead!).

"Sleepy Pete"—Every time I go to a three-day conference, there's someone sleeping in the lobby. Not waiting, not bored, but sleeping. What's he doing there?!?

"The Sport"—This is the person who goes to an event because of the quality of the golf course or the price of the stadium tickets. He or she should think about whether this is time well spent.

"The Tourist"—Some people go to an event but don't take advantage of the opportunities—they don't go to any of the seminars, they don't talk, they're not networking. Where are they? They're shopping, or sightseeing, or sitting in their room checking e-mail!

"The One-Night Stand"—They set out to network, have a series of marvelous conversations, promise to send information, and then never follow up. What started out great—all those potential relationships!—simply disappears.

"The Gang"—Five people from a company stick together all night. If you are serious about networking, you need to say goodbye to your friends at the door, and then hook up with them later and compare notes.

"My old golf buddy Bill Gates"—There's a name-dropper in every crowd. They exaggerate their connection with your CEO. They're intimate friends with the speaker. They are out to impress you, not to have a relationship with you.

"Roving Eyes"—He didn't talk to you because you're unemployed. Too bad, because your old friend Chris, who always invites you to his Monday Night Football parties, is exactly the person he wants to meet.

Dangers in Your Style

The four networking styles I've described come with potential problems. Avoid exaggerated versions of your style's behavior, for example:

The Swan: With his introverted style, the swan networker can easily disappear from sight, and people can mistake this silence as lack of interest. A swan's contacts may think they've been forgotten, and let the connection lapse. The swan's hard effort to network may not be visible. Swans can compensate for their face-to-face discomfort by diligent follow-up.

The Butterfly: Butterflies can perpetrate the annoying "Roving Eyes" mistake in a group. They need to remember that "Hi, how are you? Let's do lunch!" is not a complete conversation. Slow down, butterfly; you can meet everyone in the room but you can't have a relationship with everyone, much as you might want to!

The Dolphin: While dolphins are comfortable networkers, they can get so used to all the activity that they forget how uncomfortable it is for most people. A dolphin who is just working his or her program can be shocked when other people get overwhelmed or suspicious. In order to avoid giving the wrong impression, dolphins need to separate themselves from the toxic networkers by pacing their contact with individuals, and avoid becoming overcommitted to doing favors for people.

The Lion: In the story on page 126, Hank is the toxic lion. He's obsessed with meeting Sean Jordan, and his overattention has become a turnoff. Michelle, who is a more balanced lion, kept her focus on Jordan but was smart enough to seek alternate connections along the way to meeting him; she found Diana Jasper as her connection.

As with any set of skills, good networking is a balancing act. You want to make the most of your strengths but also find ways to compensate or repair your shortcomings. As you develop a personal networking style, you'll find that networking moves out from the career realm into the rest of your life. And that's where it truly belongs, as you'll see in the next chapter.

Sarah's Interview

Sarah could tell the interview had gone well. Dawn Temple had canceled her afternoon appointments and asked Sarah to meet with several other ELH managers. Then she'd asked Sarah to interview two less experienced people, who would be on her staff if Sarah got the job. Now it was almost evening, and Dawn escorted Sarah to the lobby.

"It was good of Bridget to introduce us," Sarah said.

Dawn replied, "Bridget, Luis, George . . . all of them. You have a pretty wide circle of friends recommending you for the job."

"I'm glad they persuaded you to see me," said Sarah. "I like this place, and I'm excited by what I've heard. Not to tip my hand, but I think this job and my experience are a good fit."

"They didn't persuade me to see you. Your resume did that. They persuaded me to look deeper than your resume. They told me about how well you handle stress, and how far they think you could go at ELH. They told me your stories. And not to tip my hand, but I liked what I heard from them last week, and what I heard from you today." Dawn held out her hand. "Someone from Human Resources will call you by Friday."

Of all the skills you learned during a job search, networking is the most important to practice after you get a job. Think of the skills you developed: research, presentation, listening, following up on promises. You're enjoying some of those new skills, and you may be the best-informed person in town. All that hard work paid off in job interviews and finally, a job offer. Now, as you start in a new job, your great opportunity is to move networking outward into your workday, and on into the rest of your life.

People typically treat a job search as an interruption in their true careers. They learn to network well for two or three months and then drop their activity once they get a job. That's a mistake. The networking skills you built while you were in transition between jobs are too valuable to file away with those old resumes. Let's look at how you can carry your network through the transition, and where it can take you in the years ahead.

Sarah Lands

Sarah finished her fourth phone call of the evening. It had taken a week to chat personally with each of the people in her network, but the satisfaction of telling people she had landed in a great job at ELH never waned. She was happy and proud of the new position. A question, however, kept tugging at the back of her mind. She flipped open her phone and dialed Michelle's number.

"Now what?" she asked when Michelle answered.

"Now what?" Michelle repeated with a laugh. Sarah heard her repeat the question to Luis, across their small office. Michelle turned on her phone's speaker.

Sarah said, "I don't want to let the new network fall apart, but I don't see how to keep it going. Finding time was easy in the last two months, when I had all day to network, but now I'm starting back in the routine of fifty-hour workweeks."

She heard Luis say, "Tell her it's just like any other project."

Michelle said, "You probably heard that. You're a project manager, so this should be easy. You should set a goal for each week—add one new person to your network. If you stay alert, you'll find opportunities everywhere, and I can tell you where to start."

"Where?" asked Sarah.

"Right in your new company. Let's list the ten people you should meet first," said Michelle, "starting with the people you'll need to know well to do your job. If you don't know all their names today, find them out by the end of the week—ask your new boss who they are. When you network within your company, set an aggressive goal . . . let's say three people a week for two months. You'll have coffee with each one of them . . ."

Sarah wrote "People to know at ELH" in her handheld computer, and began to list names.

New Job, New Network

It's tempting to disappear into a new job. There's so much to learn, so much territory to cover, that you think you don't have time for networking anymore. But you *must* build time for this into your schedule. Not only can those networking skills sharpen your job performance, but the relationships you create and maintain can be critical to your career at the company. That's how you'll find new opportunity. That's how you'll bring talented people from your career network into your company. Remember, the chances are good you'll be ready for a new position in a few short years, and rather than start all over again, now is the time to bring your networking skills, and your career network, to your workplace and keep it going strong.

When you were first looking for work, probably 20 percent of your networking was focused on your inner circle: family, friends, and close acquaintances. Strangers and referrals probably took 80 percent of your time. In the first months of a new job, reverse that ratio: Turn 80 percent of your networking toward the inner circle of your new job. Get to know managers, colleagues, executives, vendors, and customers (the last two may be outside the company but the relationships are important, especially for sales, product, and marketing jobs). Take managers from unrelated departments to lunch and ask questions until you understand what they do.

Even if you're in sales, with a focus of expanding your contacts outside the company, you need to cultivate those internal relationships early. They'll help you understand the marketplace, the operations of your industry, and ultimately help you do your job better.

It's also good to keep in mind that you don't have to focus exclusively on business—your new colleagues have lives outside of work as well. Diane Darling, CEO, Effective Networking, suggests you bring your personal network along for the ride: "For example, when your group buys a table at a charity dinner, don't just invite people because they may become clients," says Diane. "Invite people who you think will be interesting to each other. They'll have a better time. Also, invite people who can make good introductions outside of work. It could be someone who you'd like to have on a volunteer project, or a board you're serving on. Or it might be an introduction for somebody who has lots of contacts in a town you want to be active in."

Expert networkers know there's overlap among their personal networks, career networks, and workplace networks. This cross-pollination of relationships can help all three networks flourish, and makes them great connectors! Someone who couldn't help at all in your job search may become a client or customer of your new employer. They might offer good business advice. And some contact's second cousin twice removed may even become the most productive person on your staff two years from now.

Remember the job-seeker groups you belonged to during your search.

Send an e-mail update to everyone on your A-list three months after you start your new job, and send another three months later. Always remind them that you are ready, willing, and able to help them at any time with advice and referrals.

There are many excuses to stay in touch once you land a job. In addition to telling people what you are doing, you might want to work other, less formal reasons to stay in touch into your yearly calendar. These are just follow-ups by another name, such as:

- Send holiday cards.
- Remember small considerations such as birthdays (and put them on your calendar for next year).
- When you find a news article that would be interesting to a member of your network, send it with a personal note.
- Always take someone's new job, promotion, or public distinction (like an industry award) as an opportunity to get back in touch. In that case, a congratulatory phone call is just as appropriate as an e-mail or letter.

When cultivating habits like this, you'll create your own style. Some people love to send birthday cards, and others find them too personal. Some network 90 percent by e-mail while others insist that a handwritten note is more effective. The occasions, and the form of your contacts, matter less than the consideration you put into these follow-ups. A sincere and thoughtful networking habit is what makes you stand out.

Networking as a Professional Habit

Here's an example of how a simple networking habit moves into a professional setting: Recently, I went to a holiday party where I knew nobody. I ran into a stranger—literally, we collided—near the bar. We played the usual game of "After you," but instead of letting the conversation drop, I started asking questions. It turned out she was a vice president of Human Resources for the company hosting the party—out of three hundred people in the room, I bumped into an important customer of Monster. Just by asking a stranger a question, I was able to make a personal connection with a customer.

Networking isn't just for the one single purpose of moving your career forward, and that's why you want to learn how to network gracefully in life because it will get you to new heights and different places. Think for a moment about networking outside of the context of getting a job. You'll see hundreds of ways in which you can use relationships and connections to learn, grow, and accomplish things—from surprises, like finding a guy to recane your deck chairs or a rare antique bracelet for your wife, to the most important tasks, like finding the right math tutor for your child or an alternative living situation for an aging parent. Life is rich with serendipity, but if you don't ask questions you'll never recognize or reap the benefits of those chance encounters and situations. Haphazard meetings will take place all the time, and your job is to recognize them as opportunities to build a relationship. Many will turn out to be nothing more than a nice chat, but some will turn out to be quite valuable.

Remember to use *all* your networking habits. For example, you must continue to prioritize your contacts and devote what time you have to network to the A- and B-level connections. Peter Segal of Oglevie Search in London observes, "When I first started I wanted to share everything with everybody, but now I've learned to be more circumspect. [When you're working] you have to respect your limited time. I've learned that not every meeting is equally valuable; there are A players and B players and C players and you need to network with the A players."

Networking Is Good for Your New Employer

Some people even drop their networking habits at work because they are under the misguided impression that it signals disloyalty. But actually, employees who do a lot of networking inside and outside their jobs have advantages over their non-networked colleagues and employers recognize this:

- Networking employees hear about business trends faster.
- Networked employees know the best talent outside the company when it comes time to hire; they tend to make strong referrals.
- Networked employees gain experience in phone and personal presentation.
- Networked employees identify potential customers, partners, and resources (that's one reason they make good sales reps).
- Networked employees in good companies often find out just how good their situation is, and aren't tempted to leave the first time a recruiter calls.
- Networked employees are self-starters. They seek opportunity rather than wait for it.

Keeping in Touch

Even if you have little time for making new contacts, you must protect the web of relationships you built. Remember that a network without energy is dead; you have to stay in touch. Before you start a new job, put these network maintenance activities on your calendar:

- Create a mailing list and send an updated contact info e-mail out to your network on the first day of your new job.

- Send an update to your A-list in three months, reiterating your thanks and telling a little about your new work. Describe an accomplishment that makes you proud.
- Go to a conference, presentation, or networking event in your profession within three months. Then go to another within six months.
- Within two months, contact five people from your past who you did not contact when you were networking for a job. Write each a personal note telling about your new position and inviting them to stay in touch. Tell them you're getting back in touch with many people, and offer to help them in any way you can.
- Within three months, meet with the head of recruiting at your company. Describe your networking and ask how you can help them identify candidates. Do this whether or not your company has an employee referral program.
- If you haven't joined an online career networking service, join one (or two) today, and spend at least one hour a month maintaining your online network.

You probably don't want to think about extra work when you're starting a new job, but somehow you have to get out of the on/off cycle that cuts out the heart of a good lifetime networking program. This will be especially hard for those of you who are introverted or shy, but it's up to you to maintain your network. They say that repeating a task for twenty-one days makes it a habit; what if you spent just fifteen minutes a day maintaining your network? You could easily keep your safety net strong and ready to catch you when the time comes.

Another way to keep in touch with your network is to use your mailing list to send a regularly scheduled e-mail to numerous people. You could send information, usually in the form of a newsletter, to a large group of contacts. This is what marketers call one-to-many outreach, and it's a good tool for staying in touch, especially if your new job is with a small or little-known business. Because newsletters are not focused on connecting with a job right away, they're more part of a long-term career networking habit. One caution: You have to ask permission before putting someone on your mailing list, and you'd better have something to say that will be useful to people. No professional wants to receive a note that reads like a holiday "this was our year" letter.

Ten Networking Habits

I'm a great believer in the power of habit. Over time, I've noticed ten distinctive networking habits that take you way beyond just looking for a job, and they have been built directly into the networking plan of this book.

1. Seek relationships, not just contacts.

2. Focus on referrals.

3. Work outward from trusted relationships.

4. Find ways to be helpful.

5. Take advantage of group settings.

6. Seek network connections everywhere.

7. Use Internet technologies.

8. Follow up.

9. Bring networking to every corner of your life.

10. Develop your own networking style.

Although this book focuses on career networking, I think these habits are important enough to add to any part of your life.

Applying the Program to Other Goals

As networking becomes more a life skill, it works itself into many of your goals at work and beyond. Ultimately, good networking for life is more about your attitude and habits than today's contact file, and you will begin to value your web of relationships in ways that seem to go well beyond your immediate work. From learning a new skill to fund-raising for charity, most of your valuable activities benefit from a strong web of relationships. Most people find that a networking habit works its way into other interests—hobbies, parenting, lifelong dreams.

Your continued participation in associations and events broadens your scope, your expertise, and your influence. For example, if one of your goals is to become known as an expert in your field, your reputation will grow by your contact with others and your willingness to advance the field as a whole. In time, your relationships provide opportunities to publish, speak, and serve your profession. You can see this as self-serving or as selfless, but however you view it, you're becoming known.

Good networkers tell me that mastering positive habits helped them overcome their reluctance to get in touch with old friends, classmates, and acquaintances. Whether they were shy or embarrassed that they fell out of touch, the momentum that career networking generates spills over into your personal life.

Sometimes a job search concludes with self-employment. This book has concentrated on habits that bring you together with job opportunities, but networking techniques are even more valuable for the free-agent economy. Whatever a self-employed person does, he or she has to find a customer, and your career network is full of potential customers. If you have been networking for a job and then decide that free agency is a better alternative, don't be shy about alerting your network to your decision. It's a good excuse for another message to your entire web of relationships: "I've decided to go out on my own and these are the customers I'll be serving. . . . I'm asking my network for referrals to these types of customers."

When you network to get a job, the goal is obvious: a job. When networking moves into other parts of your life, how do you know it's working? Look for these outward signs that tell you networking has come into your life for good:

- When people return your calls—more than once.
- When network contacts call you for advice, connections, and ideas.
- When people think of you as a connector, not just a connection.

- When you bring people together and hear later that good things happened.
- When you connect people regularly, without expecting immediate reward.
- When it's part of your daily or weekly routine.
- When you move from making single connections to becoming a "consultant" to many different groups, from departments in your company to local charities.

EXERCISE 12

The Next Goal

Today, you're working hard at managing your career, and soon you'll get that great job! Today is a great time to imagine what networking can do for the rest of your life.

Choose a noncareer life goal that you want to reach, for example: "I will earn that graduate degree in five years" or "I am going to bring someone special into my life this year."

Write it here: _____

Now, return to the habits on page 146 and techniques throughout the book, and write how you may apply them to your goal. Focus on real, concrete actions you can take. The more detail you write, the clearer your vision of attaining that goal will be. For example:

Goal: I will earn that graduate degree in five years.

Networking to-dos:

- I will tell my personal and career networks that I am seeking referrals to graduate students, professors, and people with that degree about their experience.

- I will investigate (and join, if possible) associations that put me in touch with graduate students, professors, and people with that degree.

- I will locate and talk to a person who can describe a five-year financial strategy to pay for graduate school.

- I will explore online learning options, and locate people who have earned the degree online.

- I will locate and attend several live events focused on the area of study this year.

If you are clear in your own mind about what you want to achieve, you will find valuable connections right now in your career networking that can help you with this additional life goal.

Two Months Later

Sarah had been in her new job for two months, and tonight she had hosted a dinner to celebrate three landmarks: her new job, Martin's promotion, and a big new deal that Michelle and Luis had recently landed. After dinner, the four sat drinking coffee in Sarah's breakfast nook. Sarah and Michelle talked. Martin fiddled with his PDA, getting ready to show a new game he'd downloaded that morning. Luis had pulled a legal pad from his briefcase and doodled intensely.

Reflecting on the past few months, Sarah posed a question to Michelle. "Now that I've got the networking habit, is there anything you can think of that I should change?"

Michelle asked, "Did you have something specific in mind?"

Sarah did. "I'm great at meeting people—I've already sat down with nineteen colleagues at work—but it's such a struggle to keep good notes about who I've talked to and when I should follow up."

"That's because you're a butterfly," said Michelle.

"Socially, but at work I'm totally responsible," Sarah reacted.

"Of course you are—what I mean is that you naturally move quickly from place to place, just like a butterfly. It takes extra effort for you to settle down and spend a lot of time with someone. Tell me," Michelle continued, "isn't your biggest strength at work the fact that you can keep in touch with twenty people every day?"

"Yes, I admit that's true," said Sarah.

Luis looked up from his legal pad, and interjected, "This is a strength, Sarah. We call you a butterfly just to describe your style." He continued, gesturing to Martin with a pencil, "Martin here is what we call a swan. He likes to stay in his own pond and stick with his own kind. That's why you find those meet-and-greet events agonizing, isn't it?"

Martin smiled, his eyes darting around the screen of his PDA. "Yup. I'd rather e-mail twenty people than talk face-to-face with one. Of course, this is more fun than networking."

"Which is why you've been so effective networking via e-mail," said Luis. "Whereas Sarah, here, is much better on the phone or face-to-face."

"I get it," said Martin. "So which are you—a butterfly or a swan?"

"Neither," Luis replied. "I call myself a dolphin, because I like to cultivate deep relationships with a lot of people. For me, networking is more a way of life than a project. Michelle here is a lion—she's incredible at forming long-term relationships with a few key people. That's one reason she's so good at closing a customer—they see we're really paying attention to them."

Luis held up the pad. "Here it is," he said. "The little web that we all worked up over just a few weeks":

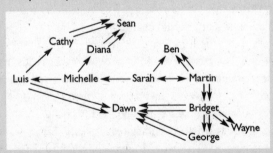

Luis concluded, "That's just what I know about this story— people, relationships, connections. Kind of simple when you look at it, but none of us could have predicted it would turn out exactly this way."

Michelle studied the drawing. "Hey, you left out toxic Hank," she said, grinning.

"Toxic Hank left himself out," said Luis.

Martin looked up from his PDA. "Oh, did I tell you that Ben and Cathy knew each other at St. Clair software?" He took Luis's pencil and added the connection.

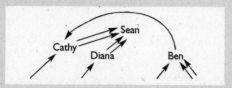

Luis responded, "I probably left out a dozen connections; these are the ones I could remember tonight."

Sarah rose to get more coffee. "We're good," she said. "Together, we could conquer the world."

"A little part of it, anyway," said Michelle. "You found a job, Luis and I found a client, Martin found a boss. The point is, none of us did it on his or her own. We're all in this together."

Y ou don't have to change your basic nature to do this work. Just like your career, networking works best when you apply your best skills most of the time. If you're a very outgoing person, then you're effective going to places where there's lots of people and just talking to everyone. If you're not an outgoing person, then your best strategy might be just going from connection to connection by e-mail.

Some of this work will come easily to you; other specific actions will be very difficult. Everyone brings a unique combination of strengths and shortcomings to career networking. Truly effective people concentrate on their strengths and compensate for their weaknesses.

I love meeting new people. I'm genuinely interested in the details of their lives, and I try to interact with every new person I meet—at a conference, in the elevator, in a store. I have a lot of lion and butterfly elements in my networking style.

I'm better at the face-to-face part of networking than the data-organizing part, and I'm lucky enough to work with a full-time executive assistant who keeps the business cards I gather organized. If your natural inclinations are similar to mine, you should at least establish a system of managing your contacts that will allow you to concentrate on your networking strength—meeting people and getting new information.

Let's say you have the opposite style, you're more like Martin the swan. You can build a tightly organized database of all sixty-five contacts in your life, but it is sheer agony for you to pick up the phone or attend a formal networking event. You don't know how to dress or what to say. Even if you go to a conference, you talk only to the one person you already know. You're going to have to compensate for that introversion, perhaps by attending events with a more extroverted friend who promises to introduce you to five new people ("Bob, I want you to meet my friend Steve, who's the best Java programmer I've ever seen").

You still have to go through the basic steps of networking—starting close to home, getting face-to-face, asking for referrals, and following up—but knowing your own strengths and weaknesses can help you create an individual networking style.

The Four Networking Styles

As mentioned in chapter 1, the swan, the butterfly, the dolphin, and the lion are metaphors for different kinds of networkers. They represent different combinations of two essential qualities of networking: how many contacts you make, and how intensely you mine those networking relationships. When you create a standard quadrant chart along these two qualities, it looks like the illustration on page 155.

Look at the four quadrants: remember that the two critical factors are the number of networking relationships you engage in, and the intensity of those relationships.

Low number/Low intensity: The Swan

High number/low intensity: The Butterfly

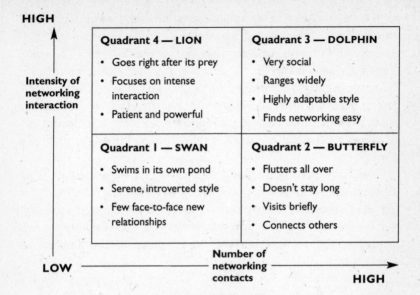

High number/high intensity: The Dolphin

Low number/high intensity: The Lion

For example, someone who concentrates on making a strong impression (high intensity) to just a few contacts (low number) exemplifies the Lion style.

I'm not a clinical psychologist—or a zoologist, for that matter—but I hope you'll see some of your own natural inclinations in these four archetypes, because they're a vehicle for understanding your strengths and shortcomings as a networker. That understanding can lead you to creating your own style—one that you'll stick with throughout your career. And career networking is a project that should never end.

Are you introverted? You're probably a bit of a swan when it comes to networking. Are you a "born salesman" in the old-fashioned sense of dialing-and-smiling a hundred times a day? You might recognize the characteristics of a butterfly. Almost nobody identifies completely with a single type; you'll probably see something of yourself in two or even three of these networking animals.

Let's stay practical and remember that we're talking about *behavior*. Your basic personality is not going to change because you read a book about career networking, and it doesn't have to for you to be effective. You can, however, identify behaviors that increase your ability to network toward a better job, and be much more successful.

Here's more detail about each style. Do you identify with any of these?

The Swan is composed and appears serene, even majestic, as it paddles around in its own pond. Although sociable, a swan mates for life, sticking close to its partner and its habitat. When swans migrate, they fly high with long, steady, slow wing beats. Then they settle down in a new pond. Swans can make a variety of sounds, but they are often silent.

Do you tend to stay in your own pond, happy with a small number of contacts? Are you rather private about yourself, and reluctant to blow your own horn unless you're with your own type? You're a swan.

As a swan-type career networker, your challenge is to get out of your pond a bit and learn to blow your own horn. The privacy and low number of your contacts can mean that you are very effective at your work, but getting connected in a meaningful way with the people who can hire you is a challenge. E-mail has been a huge gift to swan-type networkers, who tend to relate more comfortably at a distance.

At a networking event, you might be the latch-on-type of networker, who finds one simpatico person and spends the entire evening talking to them. Even though there are fifty people you should meet, you never drift outside of your comfort zone for a second. This limits the possibilities to your own "pond," so you'll need to find ways to mix it up with other species.

The swan style exemplifies qualities like:

- Loyalty.
- Predictability.
- Steady work habits.
- A good appearance.

- Serenity.
- Listening skills.

The potential downside of a swan style includes:

- Sticking with a narrow range of relationships.
- Not placing limits on unproductive relationships.
- Becoming receptive to the help of others (e.g., making connections).
- Confusing "contact" with "relationship."

The Butterfly flies from one flower to another, and never spends much time in one place. It ranges alone over a broad area, cross-pollinating all the places it visits. Butterflies are delightful—a flash of color in the room.

The networking butterfly connects with ease to many different people, but even though she looks good, she doesn't stay long enough to leave a strong impression. The good news is, a butterfly finds it easy to get out there and make things happen. Her challenge is to continue and deepen contacts past a single visit—to transform momentary contact into working career relationships. Overall, her networking lacks depth and the network value of deeper connections.

Networking butterflies love to meet new people, but in their enthusiasm for making connections, they don't always turn those meetings into significant connections. It takes a little extra effort for a butterfly to stay disciplined about the all-important follow-up, and for that reason, simple contact-management software can be a real help. Features like periodic reminders and detailed note taking can help the butterfly follow up with carefully thought-out ideas.

At a networking event, a butterfly might have that roving-eye problem . . . you're talking to one person and looking around the room. Eye contact isn't always comfortable. The other challenge of the butterfly is not to make too many commitments! In an effort to impress or ingratiate yourself to as many people as possible, you can overwhelm yourself with career relationships and disappoint people because you can't possibly follow through on all those commitments.

The butterfly style exemplifies these qualities:

- Ranges far and wide.
- Communicates with ease.
- Moves easily from one task or idea to another.
- Enjoys meeting new people.
- Enjoys making connections among people.

The potential downside of a butterfly style includes:

- By not following through on commitments, can be seen as unreliable.
- Unclear about needs—everybody knows them but nobody knows enough to help.
- Too action oriented: can lead to not doing homework before a meeting, impulsive promises, overdependence.
- Treating every connection as equally valuable.

The Dolphin is very social, a fast and powerful swimmer, very playful, and very intelligent. Dolphins also exhibit a lot of interpersonal talents: the dolphin is friendly even with other species. Communication is a big strength, and others recognize the dolphin's ability to connect. They communicate more by sound than sight; the familiar dolphin's "talking" can be heard by its group over a long range. They navigate partly by echolocation, that is, partly by bouncing sounds off distant objects. Socially, the familiar bottlenose dolphin (see: Flipper) bonds closely with a few individuals, and also belongs to larger groups whose members come and go.

If you've ever met a networking dolphin, you remember him or her. Networking dolphins balance high-quality relationships with numerous contacts. They are gregarious, with a wide range and a need to connect. The dolphin's challenge is focus—with such an ability to move on to new things, they need to remember that sticking with a course of action, even when it's a little mundane, is also key to effectiveness.

If there's a drawback to the dolphin's networking style, it may be that they don't swim in a world that's used to this combination of high quality and high number of relationships. They risk being disappointed by the lesser abilities of others to connect or follow through. Also, while dolphin-style networking is an ideal career habit, there is such a thing as getting the job. This natural networker needs to understand that networking isn't the answer to every business challenge, and sometimes she or he needs to exercise self-control when it comes to turning off the constant networking habit.

At a networking event, the dolphin arrives with a plan to make several high-quality contacts that may turn into high-quality relationships. The dolphin does this frequently and with confidence.

The dolphin style exemplifies these qualities:

- Friendly—engages people with ease.
- "Bounces off" other people in conversation—puts focus on others.
- Combines high-quality relationships with large number of relationships.
- Mixes well with other "species" of networkers.

The potential downside of a dolphin style includes:

- The building of relationships can become the goal in itself, taking focus off career goals or other essential job search work (e.g., writing a resume, searching job opportunities online).
- May be less clear to others about seeking referrals.
- May be perceived as "all things to all people" and thus not create a sense of urgency in others to help.

The Lion easily hunts alone but is also very social. The lion stalks big game with care, and even though only one in four hunts is successful, it brings home the big prey. It learns its territory carefully, even to the extent of keeping other lions away. While it can move stealthily, everyone can hear the lion when it decides to roar!

The networking lion is an exemplar of competence, intelligence, and targeted effectiveness, and has a great ability to focus on what they can get out of an encounter. If you're a networking lion, your challenge is that you can intimidate all the other creatures around you as you stalk your kill, and at a networking event, the lion might be the latch-on-type networker, the one who spends the entire evening with the one person he came to meet and ignores many other potentially important persons. The lion may need to rove around a little, taking a lesson from the butterfly, who allows serendipity to play its part.

Career counselor Peter Vogt exemplifies the lion style when he says, "I'm an introvert. I'd rather have five super good friends than fifty acquaintances, and my networking reflects that."

The lion style exemplifies qualities like:

- Confidence.
- Focused on the "big prey" (the person who can hire them).
- Leaves a clear impression.
- Leadership skills—persuasive, authoritative, accountable.

The potential downside of a lion style includes:

- Overwhelming relationships—working every relationship into "networking fatigue."
- Others mistake competence for arrogance or overconfidence.
- Underuse of serendipity—not following up on relationships that seem, at first, to offer little in the way of greater referrals.

Which Is the Ideal Style?

The ideal networking style is . . . the one you can stick with. Swans, butterflies, dolphins, and lions—all can be effective. Since you're a complicated human being, you're probably a blend of the strengths and shortcomings these archetypes represent. Maybe you'll identify in some way with each of these types.

You may ask yourself, "How much time do I focus on my strengths and how much on shoring up my weaknesses?" There's no single way to answer that because the question's too broad. The right question to ask is, "What habits or attitudes are holding back my growth as a networker, and how can I change them?"

Networking for life is really a matter of creating an individual style that makes the most of your strengths and compensates for your weaknesses. You can adopt behaviors and traits from others to become a more effective networker. You can team up with different types, like the characters in this book, to make the most of your different strengths.

When I appear at a conference as a speaker, I act like the butterfly. I fly in and out in a single day. I try to touch as many people as possible in less than an hour of speaking, and a little conversation. When I attend a conference as a participant, however, my goal is to meet at least one new person and really establish a relationship with him or her. At this point in my career, I feel that if I've really connected with two people at a conference, I've done a lot with my two days. So by connecting closely with just one or two quality people, I'm exercising the lion in me as well.

Sometimes your role at work demands a certain style. I have to move very fast in my job and meet a lot of people each week. I have some skill at this, so I have picked a butterfly existence; it's not perfect for me because executives often experience the problems of the butterfly role (even if they're another type).

When Monster was just 100 people I knew everybody's name. Then we grew, and I had to spend more time on the road meeting new people. At 5,000 people, I still know 100 people well, but not all 5,000. Sometimes I introduce myself to someone in the elevator and they say, "Yes, you introduced yourself two weeks ago." Ouch. It's very difficult in my situation to find the time to sit down and really develop a relationship with somebody new. I have to remind myself these days to make time for the lion role to develop those relationships.

As a career networker, you want to adapt characteristics from all these examples. Like the lion, you want stability and you want to be accountable for what you say. Like the swan, you also want to maintain a level of privacy and personal serenity through all this meet-and-greet. Like the butterfly, you want to expand your contacts, and like the dolphin, you can seek balance between numbers and intensity. Whatever your style, translate your strengths into action steps:

- If you enjoy going to association meetings, then list the three associations that are most appropriate for your career. Go to one event a month.

- If you do a good job at block parties, then plan on talking to at least six people at the block party about their careers (not just about what's happening on the soccer field).
- If you spend most of your time at kids' sporting practices, then instead of going out to your car and reading the paper plan on addressing one new relationship each time you go to practice.
- If you're really good with Internet tools, master them and then share what you know with less technically inclined networkers you know.

Last Note: Expand Your Comfort Zone

When you step outside of your comfort zone, you find that your comfort zone expands. When you do it over and over, you'll find yourself taking confident action—creating a large and vibrant web of relationships around your career and your life.

What's the worst that can happen? That people will reject you? Well, that's going to happen anyway, whether you nurture a strong web of relationships or not. One point of creating a strong career network is that in the process, you build up relationships that you can rely on when your ego gets bruised. Among your trusted professional relationships there will be people who can say, "Yeah, they rejected you, and that stinks. Now come with me to the Chamber of Commerce meeting tomorrow, I know someone you should meet . . ."

If you stay in your comfort zone, your web of relationships won't start humming with new referrals and new job opportunities. If you step outside it, and learn how to be comfortable outside it, well, you're not *outside* of your comfort zone anymore, are you? You've just succeeded in *expanding* it. That's what networking is all about— expanding your comfort zone. So whether you're a dolphin or a swan, a lion or a butterfly, you can learn to effectively career network in your own style and at your own pace. Get out into the world and make your career dreams come true.

Connect!

INDEX

opportunities
   finding networking, 107–108
   networkers seeking, 144
organization skills, of lion, 28–29
organizing, network file system,
    29–33
overfamiliarity, error of, 128

pack, standing out from, 5–6
partners, identifying potential,
    144
payoff, for offering help, 22–23
PDAs, keeping contact files in, 32
Pendergast, Jim, 25–26
people. *See also* contacts; referrals
   connecting with, 9–10
   excuse of not knowing, 12
   naming five you know, 25
perseverance
   at networking events, 83
   versus pestering, 127
personal brand statement
   creating, 34–35
   overrehearsed, 128
   presenting with attitude/
     enthusiasm, 35–36
   sharing in networking meeting, 48
   value of, 28, 33
personal organizer, keeping contact
    files in, 32
personal showcase, professional
    associations of, 91–92
personal Web sites
   posting resumes on, 114
   value of, 115–116
personality style
   creating comfort list and, 43
   creating relationships and,
    149–151
   identifying, 2–3
   Internetworking and, 112
   meeting agenda and, 54–55

networking event tips for, 80–81
networking qualities and, 154–160
overview, 2
playing to strengths of, 160–162
potential problems of, 135–136
strengths of, offering help and,
    23–24
working within own, 153–154
pestering, toxic networkers and, 127
phone calls
   advantage of over Internet, 121
   follow-up strategy and, 59
   long-distance networking with,
    102
   overfamiliarity and, 128
   rehearsing with comfort network,
    41–42
   speed of e-mail replacing, 111
   "warming" cold, 104–105
planning
   ahead, importance of, 77–78
   time for networking tasks, 29
planning skills, of lion, 28–29
possibilities
   opening up new, 6
   potential job, 68–69
power
   excuse of lacking, 13
   of human relationships, 17–19
prejudices, avoiding on Internet,
    121–122
preparing
   networking kit, 84
   for networking meeting, 51
   for referral meeting, 57
principles of encouraging referrals,
    19–20
prioritizing, contact list, 64–65, 131
professional assets, describing, 24
professional associations
   online communities of, 119
   overview, 90–92

professions, job networking groups
    specializing in, 96
Project Management Institute, The,
    Web site, 121
Psychology of Sales Call Reluctance,
    The (Dudley/Goodson), 24
purpose
    of national networking
        organizations, 93
    of networking events, 82–83

qualities
    of networking, measuring,
        154–155
    of networking program, 10–11
questions
    asking research and referral in
        meetings, 49–51
    networking event conversation
        topics, 79–80

rapport, establishing with
    networking meeting, 48
recruiters, using referrals, 21–22
recruitment staff, training to
    network, 21
referral list, making, 25
referral meetings
    importance of following up on,
        58–59
    managing, 57–58
referrals
    asking for in meetings, 49–51
    contacting, 55–56
    employers using, 20–21
    following up on meetings with,
        58–61
    following up with, 46
    generating, 19–20
    getting to target employers, 88–89
    from informational interviews, 63
    limitations in making, 65

making connections and, 18–19
managing bad, 131–132
meeting with, 57–58
from networked employees,
    144
organizing multiple, 101
principles encouraging, 19–20
recruiters using, 21–22
refocusing on at end of meetings,
    53–54
researching/contacting on
    Internet, 113
rehearsing
    with comfort network, 41–42
    guidelines for meetings, 47
    meetings, 45
rejection
    coping with fear of, 78
    managing, 129–131
relationships
    building in networking meetings,
        49–52
    butterflies building, 4
    creating comfort network from
        existing, 36–41
    creating network with, 5
    developing internal, 141–143
    importance of, 7–8
    listing comfort network by,
        37–39
    maintaining with
        communication, 59–60
    as network foundation, 27
    power of, 17–19
    presenting personal brand
        statement and, 35–36
    purpose of networking events
        and, 82–83
reliability, trust and, 11
research
    on professional associations, 93
    speed of Internet, 111–112